facing frustration

facing frustration
finding fulfilment

JAMES AND NINA RYE

CROSSWAY BOOKS

CROSSWAY BOOKS
38 De Montfort Street, Leicester LE1 7GP, England

First published 1997

British Library Cataloguing in Publication Data
A catalogue record for this book is available from the British Library.

ISBN 1-85684-154-5

Set in Garamond No. 3

Typeset in Great Britain by Parker Typesetting Service, Leicester

Printed and bound in Great Britain by Cox & Wyman Ltd, Reading, Berkshire.

contents

Preface

Between the two of us, we have written five books, but this one has been the most frustrating one to write. (If you doubt us, ask our patient publishers.) After we had signed the contract, three things started to block our path. The house extension (designed to give us a room to spread our paper all over the carpet in) took twelve months, and not six; James took a new job that halved his holiday time and quadrupled his work load (at least, that is what it felt like at the time); and with James joining the leadership team of our church, both of us became increasingly involved in time-consuming (and hopefully useful) activity. We are not asking for sympathy, but we want you to know that this book has been written as we ourselves have had to test the reality of what we know to be true. We write as those who are still travelling, not as those who have arrived.

Those of you who are familiar with the excellent Christian books on people and counselling by the

American clinical psychologist Dr Lawrence Crabb will be aware of the intellectual debt we owe him, particularly in the core chapters 2 and 3. While the mistakes are ours, we wouldn't want to pretend that the helpful framework for thinking about emotions and beliefs is.

All the case studies in the book have been constructed to illustrate important points. Every one of them is based on real people and situations that we have known. In order to preserve anonymity, however, we have changed details. Readers who think they can identify the originals are wasting their time. They'll only get frustrated.

King's Lynn   *James and Nina Rye*
April 1996

chapter one

The traffic jams of life

'Why aren't we moving, Daddy?' asked one of our two children for what seemed like the twentieth time in the last ten minutes. The weather outside the car was merely hot, but the discontentment thermometer inside was about to go over boiling point. How much longer would we have to wait?

It was noon in mid-August and we were on a main road in Somerset trying to reach relatives. We should have been there over an hour ago, and even if we could have got moving, there was still another twenty minutes of driving at least. But we couldn't move. That was the problem! We had turned a bend and suddenly found ourselves stuck in a line of traffic that stretched in front of us as far as the eye could see.

In the back seat the questions turned to whines and tears. In the front seats the perspiration dripped. What was happening? Why was the road blocked? Why was nobody apparently doing anything or telling us anything? Why weren't there diversion signs? Why weren't the children more understanding? And why did it have to be so sunny?

In the end we took a risk, got out the maps, turned off the main road, and continued our journey along beautiful country lanes. Somehow the fact that we would be late seemed less important. We were now moving in the right direction, and this helped to ease the tension.

Looking back, the frustration we felt over something relatively trivial now seems childish. That experience, however, was all too real, and it serves as a useful starting-point for understanding what frustration is.

Quite simply, frustration is the state of anguish that we can experience when something blocks our path and prevents us from following a particular route.

Sometimes the things blocking our route are very big: perhaps a change of boss stops the promotion we had been looking for; a broken relationship blocks the immediate path to marriage and sexual fulfilment; redundancy ruins the kind of lifestyle we had been hoping to continue to enjoy; or illness radically alters the quality of retirement we had wanted. At other times the obstacles seem comparatively small to somebody else, even though, for reasons we don't quite under-stand, they still seem so large to us: a daughter who stands in front of a mirror for 'hours', brushing her hair, and prevents us from arriving at church at least fifteen minutes before the start of the service; a colleague who is slow to change; a congregation that doesn't appear to respond to preaching. These things stop us in our tracks, and we feel various degrees of frustration as the momentum of our desires continues to try to push us into the brick wall that has suddenly appeared on the planned route of what we want.

A *three-legged stool*

If frustration is the anguish we feel when we cannot reach our goals, there are at least three factors which contribute to the intensity of the feeling we experience. Although these factors will be addressed more fully in the remainder of this book, we want to introduce them here. Understanding them provides a key to finding God at work in frustrating circumstances.

I *have to go this way*

The first factor to influence frustration is a strong belief that we must reach a particular goal. The stronger the belief, the more intense the frustration whenever our path to that goal is blocked. There is, of course, nothing wrong with having biblical goals and with making plans. The problem comes when we hold on to them too tightly. The greatest frustrations are generated when we are prevented from achieving something that we have told ourselves we *must* do in order to be significant and accepted (something that will make us feel worth while as people).

For example, consider two men who have absorbed different beliefs about what they have to do in order to

11

be significant and secure. They will be frustrated by different things. The first man, who believes that his level of income is an indicator of his success and value as a person, will be extremely frustrated by lack of promotion. The second, who is seeking significance and security in being a perfect father, will be intensely frustrated by a rebellious teenager. Both men experience the painful emotion, but for different reasons.

Natasha and Michael discovered, after two years of 'trying', that they couldn't have children. Medical tests showed quite conclusively that, short of a miracle, they would never produce offspring. After the initial shock, and during an extended period of mourning the loss of potential parenthood, they both experienced intense frustration. Natasha had been the eldest sister in a large family and had spent much of her childhood helping to look after younger siblings. Her experience of family life had helped to develop a strong belief that being a successful wife and a significant person meant having children. Having married, the route seemed clear. At an appropriate time she would give up her career and start a family. Like all of us at times, she thought she could see the end from the beginning.

But now an unexpected landslide blocked her road and, as far as Natasha was concerned, it was threatening her view of the Son as well. Michael tried to put on a brave face, but Natasha found it difficult pretending. She found herself angry and confused and depressed. She felt a physical gnawing inside her, eating at her ability to carry on. The smallest thing started her crying. And suddenly both of them became acutely aware of babies. They hadn't really noticed it before, but now it seemed that the whole world was full of babies, and 'everybody' was pregnant, except Natasha. Buying baby clothes, and then presenting them at Christmas to her sister who had just had her second child, was particularly traumatic. The memory of that time was painful for many years.

And where was God in all this? At first Natasha had tried to pray, but found herself weeping every time she tried to talk to God. She searched her soul and her history, trying to find something or someone to blame. Was she being punished? As time went on, she became angry with God for seemingly depriving her of the thing she wanted most.

It wasn't until the landslide initially stopped Jonathan's journey that he realized how much he had wanted to keep travelling down his particular road. For several years he had been on the conveyor-belt of schooling. Although his recent examination results were good, they weren't good enough for him to gain a place at the university of his choice in the year that he wanted. In front of his friends he could joke about how his 'failure' was a mixed blessing, but at night, he cried in grief and frustration because he thought *he* was a failure. He was depending on following a particular route to achieve a measure of self-worth.

The blockages we encounter force us to face up to what is important to us. Because of this, frustration can be a useful tool that helps us to explore what God could be saying to us about our values. We say: 'We have to go this way!' When we are frustrated God may be asking:

'Why do you have to go this way? Is it right that it is *so* important to you?' Are we continually frustrated about money? Perhaps God wants to challenge a subconscious belief that we have to have 'enough' of it in order to feel significant and secure. Are we frequently frustrated with others? Perhaps we have a mistaken belief that we always have to be in control.

I have to achieve this now!

A second factor influencing the intensity of frustration we feel is a belief that working to *our* timetable is crucial. Our strength of feeling is related to whether or not we believe we have to achieve a certain goal by a particular hour, day, month, or year. A person who believes that he must get married by the age of twenty is likely to feel more frustrated on his twentieth birthday, if he has failed to achieve that goal, than someone who is prepared to wait until he is eighty (if necessary) and is even prepared to forsake that goal. A Christian worker in her fifties is naturally more likely to feel frustrated than she did in her twenties when an indifferent congregation fails to enthusiastically support what God has laid on her heart. She now feels that her time is running out.

Just as frustration can be a means by which God questions our fundamental beliefs about what is important to us, so it can also be a means by which God challenges and strengthens our faith in him as well as developing our character. We say to God: 'I have to achieve this *now!*' And God prompts us to reflect on whether or not we really trust in his sovereign power and perfect timing as he seeks to build patience in us. At the death and raising of Lazarus (John 11:1—44) the disciples were powerfully reminded that God would operate his own timetable, despite their well-intentioned desires to plan events.

It shouldn't happen to me

A third and subtle factor which contributes to the intensity of frustration we feel is a naïve belief that route blockages shouldn't happen to Christians, especially ones who are as 'mature' and 'full of the Spirit' as we are. Although most of us would rarely admit to it, we tend to cling to at least one, if not both, of the following two views from time to time:

- ➤ A mistaken belief that because I am special to God I am somehow immune from all the effects of living in a sinful world. Although disasters and difficulties happen to other people, God will mysteriously protect me from all danger and difficulty. My car will always start first time in the morning, there will always be a parking space, the dentist will always find my fillings in perfect condition, God will remove all nasty people from work and church so that I may work and worship in Utopia, my partner will always recognize me as the perfect companion, my children will praise me to their friends as the perfect parent, my pastor will be able to walk on water as well as fish in it, and all will be well in the world.

15

➤ A mistaken belief that if blockages stop my progress, I will be able to move *any* mountain, *almost instantly*, *on every occasion* through prayer, and continue on my journey unhindered.

When something stops our movement towards a particular goal, we feel a sense of shock and surprise, and the subsequent outrage adds to our pain. 'God, I want this Christian youth work to grow for your glory. I want what you want: the extension of your kingdom. You know my motives, and you know how much money and support we need. Why isn't it coming? Why are people deserting me? You called me to this work; why are you allowing this to happen to me?' While we are crying to God, however, he may want to use the experience to move us on to a more mature understanding of his Word and to a deeper level of discipleship.

Frustration flows when we are stopped in our tracks. And the experience can leave us facing important questions about ourselves, about God, and about the particular journey we are taking. Frustration almost certainly has more than the three underlying causes that we've introduced above, but whatever we believe or don't believe, the emotions associated with frustration are real enough. It's those feelings which are the subject of the next chapter.

chapter two

Painful emotions

Abigail had just turned thirty and was a well-liked, mature Christian, whose only obvious weakness was a shyness that made her socially awkward on occasion. In deep depression, she described something that had happened to her months previously. She felt she had lost her reputation at work.

Although she was a meticulous and able employee with a good attendance record, she was managed by a person who continually demanded what was unreasonable. Abigail had, on medical advice, taken a fortnight off work to recover from the cumulative effects of stress and over-tiredness. She had had serious headaches and depression, and had been susceptible to a number of viral infections. On returning to work, Abigail learned that her employer had judged her to be taking time off unnecessarily and had reported her to Head Office.

Abigail experienced an overwhelming sense of anger

at what had happened to her, and fear as she thought about the future. At the time, it felt as if she would have to carry this misleading assessment with her for the rest of her working life, and that wherever she turned, it would be there, harming her. She felt powerless to change what she saw as a ruined career. At night, before she was prescribed sleeping tablets, she cried into the long, dark silences about the injustice that she had suffered. Work no longer seemed a place where she felt respected and valued, and she didn't want to go there. A few attempts at finding alternative employment proved unsuccessful.

To her shame, Abigail even found herself longing to be more ill so that she could avoid going into the office she now hated. Her peers at work tried to be as reassuring as they could, and well-meaning Christian friends quoted the right texts at her and rebuked her for the anger that surfaced in her accounts of what had happened. But the anger and fear would not go away. She continued to try to meet with God out of habit and duty, hoping that her feelings would change, but now there was a numbness in the relationship. He seemed so far away as she questioned whether she really could trust him.

When we reach the state that Abigail was in, we don't immediately want a sermon. Although there are many things we could say, one of the most important things we can do initially is to acknowledge the reality of the pain. Despite the fact that many Christians are afraid of emotion and especially of emotional pain, the Bible is quite clear that there is a time to weep as well as to laugh (Ecclesiastes 3:4) and a time to mourn with those who mourn (Romans 12:15).

We are used to being taught what to believe and how to behave. We may be used to sermons and Bible studies on topics such as the work of the Holy Spirit, the fatherhood of God, heaven and hell, tithing, evangelism, and relationships. But when did your church last seriously address the issue of feelings? Perhaps in the last ten years you've heard one sermon on joy, but what about teaching on the feelings of anguish, sorrow, anger, disappointment, discontentment, and anxiety? All of these emotions are also an important part of life, are often associated with frustration, and are all addressed in the Bible.

When frustrated, we are likely to be feeling a range of emotions. These may include bitterness towards others, hatred, a desire to get even in some way, and a sense of betrayal. There could also be humiliation and anger, together with anxiety and concern for the future. When others present us with such a powerful mixture, there is a tendency to deny it, or to discourage it and hope that it will go away. 'Yes, dear, don't worry, you'll soon get over it. Time is a great healer, you know . . . Now, this is what the Bible says . . .' We don't know how to handle it, and we often have a sneaking suspicion that powerful emotion is almost always (if not always) sinful. We may even want to condemn people for feeling so strongly. Certainly in our own frustration we are often surprised by the strength of the emotion. It can catch us unawares ('Am I really *that* bitter about what has happened?'), and we might condemn ourselves for feeling anger and concern.

Some of us may have been guilty of adopting a very simplistic (and unbiblical) view of human emotion. In Christian circles there has sometimes been a view that emotions can easily be divided into two types – positive and negative – and that positive emotions such as joy are always good, and negative emotions such as anger are always bad. Just a brief, serious reflection will show that this cannot be so, however. Presumably we would want to condemn the joy almost certainly experienced by some of the Jerusalem religious leaders over the death of Jesus, and would not want to condemn Jesus for the anger that he showed on occasions.

Perhaps the label 'negative' has been strengthened by a growing awareness in the church of the link between certain powerful emotions and mental and physical health. And consequently (because we know, for example, that unrelenting bitterness and anger can sometimes contribute to a range of physical complaints such as headaches, tension, and ulcers), we want to discourage ourselves and others from feeling 'negative emotions'. We tell ourselves and our friends to stop behaving in certain ways, to start thinking in right ways, and to have more faith. This, we think, is bound to cure the problem. Such a stance, however, often leads to two further problems. First, there is the despair that we can feel when we try the above and still find ourselves facing the emotional pain (like Abigail). Secondly, such a solution may add to our distress as we try to deny the emotions that we are unmistakably feeling.

In this book we want to argue that it is sometimes legitimate for Christians to experience so-called 'negative' emotions; and, indeed, that if we didn't feel them in certain circumstances there might be something wrong with both our humanity and our Christianity. Being frustrated is an emotional experience. What we need to do is be aware of our emotions and assess them in the light of the Bible. The last thing we should do is deny their existence or always think that we have to apologize for them. We shouldn't be afraid of facing up to the fact that being frustrated can involve real, deep pain.

In his book *Understanding People*, Dr Lawrence Crabb, a Christian psychologist, describes a more useful framework for categorizing emotions. We have a tendency to label pleasant emotions as good and unpleasant emotions as bad. Frustrating events, however, always tend to generate unpleasant emotions, and it is wrong to think that the emotions associated with these events are always bad. Dr Crabb argues that it is more biblical to think of emotions as being either constructive or destructive.

Some emotions seem to interfere with what people should do – namely, love God and others – and so may properly be regarded as destructive. It is easy to see, for example, how bitterness at being denied promotion would fit into this category. Although less immediately apparent, joy could also be regarded as destructive in certain circumstances – for example, someone might experience joy at gaining advantage at the expense of others, or on taking 'sweet revenge'. In both these cases you could argue that the 'pleasant' emotion is interfering with their love for God and others, and is therefore destructive for them.

Other emotions can encourage us to reach out to God and people, and although they are sometimes traditionally labelled as 'negative' they can be extremely constructive for us. The social reformer William Wilberforce experienced anger when each attempt to introduce legislation to abolish slavery was defeated. But it drove him closer to God and increased his determination to work for the rights of his abused fellow human beings. The discontent that Nehemiah felt about the *status quo* of the Jerusalem ruins (Nehemiah 1 – 2) not only caused him to weep, but also drove him to pray fervently and plan meticulously for God's glory and for the benefit of thousands.

During any frustrating experience, we are likely to see a mixture of constructive and destructive emotions: resentment along with righteous anger; crippling guilt along with sorrow that motivates change.

Bitter resentment versus *righteous anger*

The most common emotion people experience during frustration is anger. We find ourselves angry with God, with others, and with ourselves. And there have been plenty of mild-mannered people who have been surprised to find themselves slamming a door or thumping a table before bursting into tears. If the force of the red-hot anger sometimes surprises us, we are, sadly, often too accustomed to the ice of the blue anger – the moaning and grouching, the envy and bickering, the calculated destructiveness.

Anger has had a bad press, and in many cases it has been deserved. Only a fool would try to deny that it has a destructive side which has contributed to much pain and grief. We need to take to heart the warnings of Jesus in the Sermon on the Mount about the root causes of sinful action, and make sure that our hearts don't provide the festering soil in which murderous thoughts can grow into hateful actions and words (Matthew 5:21–22). It should be clear by now, however, that we want to argue that not all of that anger is necessarily wrong.

God is portrayed as one of the angriest beings in the Bible. We are so familiar with the stories about the destructive effects of anger (for example, the murder of Abel, Potiphar's wife's denunciation of Joseph, and Jonah's sulking) that we sometimes downgrade the frequent occasions where God's anger at the sin and stubbornness of people is powerfully portrayed.

This anger is expressed by God throughout the Bible. We see it when Moses returns from collecting the Ten Commandments to find the people committing idolatry (Deuteronomy 9:8), and when Jesus twice cleanses the temple of money-changers (John 2:12–25; Mark 11:12–21). On the first of these two occasions Jesus is described as being 'eaten up' with anger (John 2:17, literally). In the opening chapters of Mark's gospel, where Jesus bursts on to the scene and provokes a strong backlash from Satan, Jesus sees the hardness of heart towards the kingdom of God, and becomes distressed and angry at it (Mark 3:5). For God, being angry is part of his holy character.

Our emotional states and attitudes of anger are evaluated by God. If we are frustrated because some of our goals have been thwarted, part of the anger we are experiencing is likely to be destructive. If it isn't recognized and confessed, it can so easily take hold of us and grow into bitterness and resentment. Suppressed anger acts like a time-bomb that will eventually explode and hurt others as well as ourselves.

If that destructive anger is directed towards ourselves, we are likely to act in a way that will hurt ourselves – as if we want to punish ourselves. Behind many cases of self-abuse (such as alcoholism or drug addiction) are a deep anger and self-hatred. If that anger is directed towards God, we may want to give up our faith, or we may start to behave in a bizarre way. A male counsellee once confessed: 'My pornography is my temper tantrum at God, because he hasn't given me a wife.' If that anger is directed towards others, we shall use our contact with them to either scorch them or freeze them in an attempt to get even. That is why Paul commands us to get rid of bitterness and rage (Ephesians 4:31).

It could be, however, that part of our anger is both legitimate and positive. It could be that our anger at the thwarting of our goals and desires was not just a proud attempt to rule our world, and to have our agenda, but was rather an expression of the kingdom of God in us. The people who were behaving badly towards us were also inflicting unnecessary pain and grief on others. The people who were blocking us were also blocking the work that God had so clearly revealed through his Word, through the wise counsel of others, and through his Spirit bearing witness to our spirit. We are angry because the values of the kingdom are being abused, and/or because the growth of the kingdom is being hindered.

It is sometimes claimed that anger is sinful immediately it is directed towards a person, but Christ's anger was directed, at times, towards the Pharisees. The moral test of anger is to ask not 'Who is that anger directed towards?' but 'What is the underlying cause?' Am I angry because I can't have my way, or am I angry because God's will is not being done? Is my anger leading me closer to God, or away from him?

Seen in this light, there are occasions when our anger and frustration can be a source of encouragement to us. In the example at the beginning of the chapter, Abigail's depression was caused in part by her desperate, guilty attempts to suppress the anger she was feeling at the way she was being abused at work. She had been taught that it was wrong for Christians to get angry. It was extremely helpful for her to be able to acknowledge her anger, and to realize that although her motives were far from totally pure, there was an element of her anger that was justified. The God of justice, Abigail's God, was also angry at the injustice of Abigail's treatment, and in being angry, Abigail was being like God. She could confess her sinful desires for hurt and revenge, without having to deny her feelings.

When we are frustrated because God's will is not done, it is sinful *not* to be angry. Television coverage of the slaughter in the former Yugoslavia, and violation of human rights there, showed an angry outburst from a UN commander standing near the burnt body of a child. The officer was visibly moved as he condemned the cruel murders of innocent civilians. He took the unusual step of publicly naming and condemning the commander of the troops known to be responsible for the atrocity. As Christians we should not condemn the anger felt on this occasion, or do spiritual gymnastics to try to suppress our own anger. Rather, we should recognize that in such circumstances, to fail to be angry would mean that we had lost touch with the heart of God.

Crippling guilt versus constructive sorrow

On occasions the frustration we feel is caused by our own sinful actions. We don't always have the luxury of blaming external circumstances or other people. All too often we carry around the stumbling-blocks within ourselves. There is a war within us. The good that we want to do doesn't always get done, and the evil that we want to avoid gets completed all too quickly. At times, when the consequences of our sin are particularly noticeable, or humiliating for us (as well as for others), the frustration is so great that we are tempted to give up.

Graham was tired of being an imperfect dad. He deeply loved his children, but recently he had done a good job of alienating them, despite this being the last thing on earth he wanted to do. He knew that he had a very short fuse, and that over the years he had developed a pattern of relating which meant that, in times of stress in the family, anger was often the first response. He had read books and prayed for help, and really wanted to be able to respond to normal family pressure in a less destructive and more loving way. But despite all this, he really blew it.

They were on a crowded beach when it happened. They had gone there to enjoy a day out. The sibling rivalry finally pushed him over the edge as the older brother pushed the younger brother just a bit too hard, causing the younger one to drop his ice-cream. Graham shouted so loudly that even he was eventually embarrassed by the embarrassment he was causing and by the words he was pouring out. As the howling children ran to their mother, he could see their fear, and he felt the pain of her accusing look. He fumed in the car all the way home and ached for days as he watched them tip-toe around him, as if treading on broken glass.

As he dried the dishes rather forcefully to express his frustration (it was more constructive than throwing them at the wall), Graham felt the pain deep within. Despite his real love, there was a crushing voice pulling at his heart, telling him to give up; telling him that he would never make it as a good father, no matter how hard he tried; telling him to leave home and let them get on with it; telling him to kill himself.

The Bible contains many examples of people who faced deep sorrow because of their sinful actions. After his adultery with Bathsheba, and the murder of her husband, David wrote:

> . . . my bones wasted away
>   through my groaning all day long
> For day and night
>   your hand was heavy upon me;
> my strength was sapped
>   as in the heat of summer.
>
> (Psalm 32:3–4)

The way to handle the crushing sorrow is not to wish it away on a whim, or to wallow in it and give up, but to understand it, limit it, and use it.

We shouldn't be surprised by the sorrow we feel over our own sinful actions. Just as our physical bodies respond to physical pain as a protective measure, so God has built us with a spiritual pain mechanism. Provided our consciences have not been abused through years of neglect, we shall feel the guilt caused by sin, and that will lead to sorrow. If it didn't, we would be behaving in a sub-Christian manner. The sorrow we feel is a mark of God's grace in our lives. It's one of his ways of speaking to us. If we feel sorrow, the emotion may be 'negative', but the signs are positive, and the experience can be constructive. The trauma of surgical intrusion may have been numbed by the anaesthesia, but post-operative distress is usually a symptom of healing.

Not only do we need a new perspective on sorrow over sin, we also need to place some clear biblical limits on it. The tears can wet the ground, but they shouldn't go on for ever, turning the mud into a quagmire which is perfect for wallowing in. The way to limit sorrow is to express it, confess it, and believe in God's forgiveness.

Children who know they are loved by their parents cope with the aftermath of wrong-doing in exactly the same way. They may cry and talk about their bad behaviour or words, but then they know that once this has happened, their parents will not go on raising the issue on every available occasion.

Sorrow that is not acknowledged is kept underground. Although we may hide our sorrow, however, it will resurface later with added force and with damaging consequences. It is most likely to show itself through a growing hardness towards God or through a lingering depression. Once sorrow is acknowledged, it can be confessed to God; and once confessed to God, it can be forgiven. After the words from the psalm quoted above, David went on to write:

> . . . I acknowledged my sin to you
> and did not cover up my iniquity.
> I said, 'I will confess
> my transgressions to the LORD' –
> and you forgave
> the guilt of my sin.
>
> (Psalm 32:5)

Sometimes we choose to believe the lies of Satan when he whispers that we have committed the unforgivable sin, or that we have put ourselves beyond the influence of God's grace because we have proved to be not good enough. Graham certainly felt he wasn't worthy to be a Christian, and that there was little point in trying any more. God, however, forgives because of his free grace, because of the finished work of Christ, because of his decision to forgive. I don't have to carry the crushing burden of my sin. Christ has already been crushed for it. John writes:

> If we confess our sins, he is faithful and just and will forgive us our sins and purify us from all unrighteousness (1 John 1:9).

By believing what God has said to be true, I am able to put a limit on the sorrow. My sorrow is an expression of grief over my actions. It should not become an attempt to punish myself for what Christ has already been punished for. I may not want to forgive myself, but what right have I to hold on to what God has declared forgiven?

The third strategy for handling sorrow is to use it constructively. Paul is able to write that he didn't regret the sorrow he had caused the Corinthian congregation, because their sorrow led them to repentance (2 Corinthians 7:8–13). They used it to bring them closer to God. Graham was experiencing something of what Paul described as 'worldly sorrow bringing death'. It was paralysing and destructive. It robbed him of hope in his relationship with his family and with God. It condemned him without motivating him to rebuild.

Later that month Graham was able to distinguish between a right sorrow for his sin and a crippling guilt that would destroy him. He confessed his sin to God and apologized to his family. And he used his sorrow constructively. The experience had brought him to a point where he realized he had a problem that wouldn't go away and for which he needed serious help. He sought out a biblical counsellor who spent several hours listening to him, enabling him to understand why he was so angry, and helping him plan various changes in his thinking and behaviour.

In this chapter we have discussed only anger and sorrow, but many (if not all) of the emotions associated with frustration can be either destructive or constructive – keeping us apart from people and from God, or bringing us into closer relationships with our Maker and with other people. The positive discontentment (Philippians 1:12–15) which refuses to accept a wrong situation, or the legitimate anguish in the face of awful circumstances (Luke 22:44) (both of which drive us closer to God) can so easily become something debilitating that can start to eat us from inside.

Frustration brings powerful feelings with it, and those emotions reflect the fact that we are human beings, made in the image of God. God has made us a chip off the old block. We feel because he feels. For too long, frustrated Christians have tried to hide their feelings or have automatically felt guilty about them, and this has led to unhealthy churches. The issue is not whether we should have such strong emotions, but whether those emotions work to help extend God's kingdom. We shouldn't be concerned because the feeling is strong, but we should evaluate it to make sure that it is being used constructively rather than destructively.

chapter three

Unhelpful beliefs

Great sobs surfaced from deep within Peter and moaned across the living-room as he tried to express the extent of the pain and frustration that he felt.

At thirty-five Peter had been a fire officer and an active sportsman, with a wife and three healthy children. Now, at forty-five, Peter was unemployed, divorced, and virtually paralysed. He lived alone, and was forced by circumstances beyond his control to stay at home all day. His only company was the bland diet of 'personalities' in quiz shows, chat shows and soaps, and the brief nightly visit from a nurse who came to wash him before putting him to bed at about 7pm.

The multiple sclerosis had progressed quite rapidly. As it became worse, Peter's anger had driven most people away, eventually including his wife, who felt unable to share Peter's suffering and bring up the children in such an atmosphere. Ten years on from that first visit to the doctor's, Peter felt that he had lost everything.

Below the surface

Below the real, surface suffering, which evoked sympathy as we watched his weak, uncoordinated attempts to plug in a kettle or open a biscuit tin, there was a terrifying despair. Here was a man who felt totally worthless, and totally unloved. The frustration he felt because of his physical restrictions was bad enough, but beneath the surface lurked a terrible loneliness and self-loathing which we started to talk about on the day he cried.

Peter may be an extreme example, but we want to argue that the vast majority of people (including the vast majority of Christians) share something of the same deep insecurities that Peter felt. All of us have two fundamental psychological needs: the need to feel significant, and the need to feel secure.

Peter felt completely insignificant because the roles through which many people traditionally find significance had been taken from him. His illness had caused him to lose his job and contributed to the loss of his family — both areas where he had been able to demonstrate some skill and creativity. He had done things at work and in the home which enabled him to leave his mark on others. Because of these things he had been able to feel that he mattered; without them, he felt lost. And without them he felt alone and insecure in a frightening world. There was no warmth of human relationship to support him, no people to whom he could run. Peter's deep desire to have these needs for significance and security met, and his inability to have them met in traditional ways, only heightened his frustration.

Although we may, in the main, succeed in keeping our own insecurities hidden, most of us have the same deep longings as Peter. It is, however, these insecurities, based on mistaken beliefs, that are the root cause of all our frustration. Changing the beliefs that cause these insecurities provides the key to starting to deal with our frustration.

Only Jesus

Christ alone is the one who is able to fully satisfy our needs for significance and security. This is one of the most liberating truths for a Christian (and sadly one that many of us fail to appreciate fully).

Ultimately my need for significance cannot be met by my work (whether paid or unpaid) or by my relationships, because circumstances may leave me unable to fulfil certain roles, and people may let me down or desert me. My need for significance can be fully met only by Christ, the unchanging one who is beyond the limitations imposed by time and a sinful world. I gain my significance, not from what I *do*, but from the fact that the Saviour of the world has decided to love me and include me in his family. I have a purpose for living because he gives me the privilege of serving in his kingdom. He frees me to work, not in order to satisfy a deep longing for significance, but in order to please him. I matter, not because in some way, through my efforts, I have left a minuscule mark on history by impinging on the lives of a few other people, but because Jesus says that I matter. My significance rests in him. And once I realize this and accept it, I no longer have to fight to secure the fact that I matter.

Although there are many alternative sources of significance that people have traditionally sought, it is possible to identify four major areas where we may have attempted to satisfy our fundamental longings. Throughout the world people are judging their significance

- ▶ by how much they earn,
- ▶ by their educational or other achievements,
- ▶ by the frequency and 'success' of their sexual activity, and
- ▶ by their 'power' to get things done and influence others.

And these same people become frustrated when circumstances prevent them from achieving their goals, and hence from meeting their needs. People who live in San Francisco know only too well that however secure the roadway may look, it will almost certainly buckle one day in an earthquake and reveal a gaping hole beneath.

Why do I matter?

At first it was difficult to understand why Mary wouldn't let go. There were things that she knew were wrong, but which she just wouldn't stop doing. As she approached forty, she was a formidable force to be reckoned with.

When Mary was in her early thirties, Jason, her husband, had suffered a serious mental breakdown. He was off work for nearly a year before eventually deciding he could not face returning to his stressful role as a teacher and middle manager in a comprehensive school. It took another eighteen months before he had enough confidence to take up a clerical position in a Post Office.

During these difficult years Mary's role within the marriage had changed considerably. In the early years of the marriage she had been the dependent one, but her husband's illness propelled her into a new role. Financial necessity forced her into part-time work (something she would not have considered before). She found herself having to make big decisions alone when her husband couldn't cope. She had to do jobs that he would normally have done for her. People began to admire her strength and the way she was learning to adapt to her difficult situation. She enjoyed a new-found status in her own right.

As Jason's health improved, however, Mary fought to maintain her new role. It wasn't that Jason wanted to repress her in any way, but he too needed to be able to do things for himself again, and pick up some of the jobs he had done before (albeit in a redefined relationship). The problem was that Mary wouldn't let go. There were times when it seemed as if Mary didn't want him to get better. When he started to do things for himself again, Mary criticized him for not doing them in the way that she would have done. She was frustrated by his progress. She seemed to be undermining his weak confidence at every stage, always chatting about his illness and what he hadn't been able to do. And the awful thing was that Mary could see the pain that she was causing, and wanted to stop.

Mary's behaviour ultimately stemmed from a mistaken belief. She was fighting so hard to hang on to what she had, and was so frustrated by having to let go, because she was looking to this new role to give her the significance that she longed for. Only as she came to see that Christ alone could give her real significance (after a period of counselling) did she have the freedom to start to let go and to lay down part of what she had been previously clutching so tightly.

The frenetic grasping for significance outside of Christ, and the subsequent frustration in failing to achieve it, can be seen everywhere.

At school, college, or university it can be seen in students who become depressed or even suicidal because they fail to achieve the marks they wanted (even though their marks may be the envy of some). 'What shall I tell my parents? What will people think of me if I don't achieve perfection?'

At work it can be seen in the frustrations of the under-promoted, who feel judged as failures because of their job title and the size of their pay-packet. 'If I were any good, we would have moved into a bigger house by now . . .' Alternatively, it can be seen in the lies of the over-promoted, who are so insecure that they feel they have to take credit for everything. 'I can't let others know that I actually didn't do that. It would threaten my position . . .'

Among the unemployed it can be seen in the self-loathing of those who feel that powerlessness and poverty must mean that they are worthless.

At church it can be seen in tenacity of those who feel they have to grasp the limelight as much as possible. It can be seen in the anger of those who feel under-used, and who need limelight and activity to feel important to God. It can also be seen in the anger of those who leave in a huff when they can't get their own way. (To stay after 'defeat' would be too humiliating.)

In the home it can be seen in the growing bitterness of the unmarried daughter who feels undervalued because of her obedience to God, or in the anger of the wife who cannot control her husband or children. 'What will people think of me?' It is horrifically seen in the violence of the abusive husband who uses outrageous force to establish ultimate control.

Look up

Billy Graham used to tell the famous story of the tightrope-walker who crossed the Niagara falls. After he achieved this amazing feat, the crowds cheered enthusiastically. When the tightrope-walker asked the crowd if they believed he could repeat the performance, but pushing a wheelbarrow, they all cried 'Yes!'

After he had done this, he asked them: 'Do you

believe I could push a person across in the wheelbarrow next time?'

And again they cried: 'Yes!'

'Who then will be the first volunteer?'

The roar of the waterfall covered the sound of their departing feet.

If we are to achieve any measure of freedom from frustration, it will involve us in walking by faith, not by sight. It will involve us in a conscious decision to get into God's wheelbarrow, and trust that what he says is true, regardless of the subtle messages that we have spent our whole lives listening to. The problem is that the waterfall roars so loudly. It is intimidating. Significance, as measured by the world, is tangible. Money can be counted, projects can be assessed, sexual activity can be experienced, power over others can be appreciated or enjoyed. Although no less real, the significance that Jesus gives is seen by faith: it lies beyond the waterfall, and at times it can seem distant unless we decide to keep it in our minds and cling on to it.

At twenty-six, Richard had had a meteoric career. He had been promoted three times since leaving university and was managing a team of twenty people in a multinational food company. He liked his work and felt that his academic knowledge and managerial skills were being utilized and developed in his job. He had the luxury of feeling fulfilled and of being very well paid for doing what he enjoyed. He and his wife Sally were also serving in a small Baptist church that was experiencing a period of rapid growth.

Everything was fine until one day Richard received a letter that caused his stomach muscles to clench and literally made him feel sick. The physical nausea spasmodically returned for the next sixth months, but the sickness of heart, caused by the insecurity resulting from the letter, was to stay with him for many years.

Richard's company was closing down its factory in his town. As a valued member of the middle-management team, Richard was offered promotion (and a bigger car) provided he agreed to move to a factory in another country.

Sally's mother had died suddenly only six months before Richard got the letter. Sally's father, Jack, who lived nearby, was in his late sixties and was beginning to show signs of extreme confusion. Richard and Sally didn't know if these were the early symptoms of some mental illness, or whether they were a side-effect of the grief that Jack was experiencing. Jack clearly wasn't coping too well and Sally didn't want to leave him so soon after her mother's death, or until she felt more confident about his health. And at the church, things were going so well. For the first time in what seemed like ages, people were being converted regularly, and Christians who moved into the area and who came to visit the church actually stayed because they liked what they saw. Both Richard and Sally were developing a respected counselling and teaching ministry. They didn't want to leave the church or the town, let alone the country – and so, after an agonizing period, Richard decided to stay put and accept redundancy.

The church prayed for them and were thrilled for

Richard when he managed to secure another job in a local electronics factory after a few months. He had less of a management role, lost his company car, and had to take a 25% cut in salary. Nevertheless, he told himself he was content, because he felt he had made a sensible decision for the right motives.

The trouble was, it took Richard years to come to terms with what had happened. Although not always consistent in his thinking, paradoxically he didn't often regret the decision he had made. He and Sally were both greatly blessed by an increasing friendship with Jack, who appreciated their care, and by continuing to see God at work in their church and through them. But for Richard, being confident he had made a good decision didn't satisfy his deepest needs. The anger and frustration that he felt weren't faced up to and dealt with, but were driven underground where they congealed into several murky pools of depression.

He was depressed when people younger than him started to get promotion above him into jobs which he felt he could easily do. He missed the kudos of being part of the 'inside', the management team. It hurt him to see people of his age with bigger houses and cars than he had, especially when he told himself what he might have been earning if he had stayed in his former job. He avoided school or university reunions because he didn't want his 'failure' to be exposed to his peers. Despite an outwardly 'successful' and obedient Christian life, Richard was still clinging to a false belief.

And as if all this wasn't enough, Richard also 'lost' his church (one of the reasons he had stayed in the first place). There was a scandal, a moment of weakness; and the pastor thought it best if Richard and Sally left because of the other people involved. Overnight, Richard appeared to have lost several friends and a ministry that God had been so clearly blessing. He sank into depression. Although they joined another church, it would be years before he and Sally felt 'useful' again.

We wish there was a happy ending to this story, but in a sense, the ending is still being written. Richard is now much more at peace with himself and with God than he was five years ago. If you talk to him about it, he will tell you that he is repenting, trying to change his faulty thinking; but that repentance is an ongoing process. The tangible things that he used to look to as sources of security are constantly before him, almost mocking him with what he hasn't got.

Richard has learned that here is an area where he has to walk by faith, not by sight. The tape playing in his head says: 'Look at you. You're a failure because you haven't got X and Y . . . Go on, get frustrated as you long for the things that you need . . .' He has to constantly replace this with a tape which says: 'You matter to God. You may want these things, but you do not need them. God chose you in Christ before you could do anything (Ephesians 1:4). Whether you have riches or poverty, service or ease, you have significance because of him and his will, and not because of things or achievements. When the world judges you, it is using worldly values. Learn not to be threatened by what you haven't got, or by what you're not doing (provided, of course, you would be willing if he gave you the opportunity).' Like Noah, Richard has to exercise faith, believing God's word in a culture which says that real significance is to be found elsewhere.

Security

Christ is the source of our ultimate security, as well as of our ultimate significance. As Christians, we know the texts:

> God demonstrates his own love for us in this:
> while we were still sinners, Christ died for us
> . . . Who shall separate us from the love of
> Christ? Shall trouble or hardship or persecution
> or famine or nakedness or danger or sword? . . .
> For I am convinced that neither death nor life,
> neither angels nor demons, neither the present
> nor the future, nor any powers, neither height
> nor depth, nor anything else in all creation, will
> be able to separate us from the love of God that
> is in Christ Jesus our Lord (Romans 5:8; 8:35,
> 38–39).

And yet, despite such powerful statements of the unconditional and everlasting love of Christ for us, and despite a clear demonstration of that love on the cross, there are times when it doesn't seem enough for us. There is, of course, nothing wrong in wanting other people to love us. God did not make us to be alone, and often the love of Christ can be experienced through the kindness and compassion shown by others towards us. As the body of Christ on earth, the church should be demonstrating the love of Christ to individuals in tangible ways. But there are times when we crave other people's affection with an intensity which suggests that we need others to fulfil a longing to feel secure. At times we seem unable to put our desire to receive human love into perspective. We seem unable to let the strong, eternal love of Christ provide us with the security for eternity that we need. We persist in looking to human love to meet our ultimate needs, and for a while we may be content. But when others can't, or don't give us that love, instead of drinking from the unquenchable fountain, we start shouting at the dried-up stream.

If a consequence of my failing to let God meet my need for significance is a desire for power and achievement, a consequence of my failing to let God meet my need for security is a craving for pleasure and comfort. And just as a long-term, unfulfilled lust for power can lead to violence (in a frantic attempt to meet the need to control), so a long-term, unfulfilled yearning for pleasure and comfort can lead to all kinds of immorality and destructive behaviour. If people won't give me the love I need, I may try resort to all kinds of deceit to get that love; and if that fails, I shall have to fill the gaping void with something or somebody to stop me facing the pain.

At twenty-four Sara and Martin were heading for a divorce. They had known each other since they were fourteen, when they met at church. They had got married when they were nineteen. Samantha, their daughter, was born six months after the wedding; Susie

45

two years later; and Joe fourteen months after that. When they got married they had quite normal expectations. They both wanted to love each other, and each hoped the other would help to meet the usual emotional and physical needs. Sara planned to lead a fulfilled and happy life as a mother, and Martin wanted a sympathetic homemaker and lover. Both of them, however, found that part of the intended route to their happiness (the children) actually became part of the obstacle as well.

Sara became constantly tired and preoccupied with trying to meet the needs of the children. Although she still loved Martin, he felt that his physical and emotional needs were no longer important to Sara and he started to withdraw into himself. She became even more distant, but, at the same time, felt that her own emotional and physical needs were being ignored by him. Martin's affair with Kim at work almost seemed inevitable. She had provided friendship when his wife seemed too boring, too tired, and too busy to care; and this emotional dependency eventually led to various illicit sexual encounters, which were eventually discovered. Both Martin and Sara were frustrated by each other's behaviour, and could see little hope of trying to rebuild a marriage in which they would apparently receive little love.

We don't want to trivialize the difficult situation they were in. At the heart of their problem, however, was a belief that their ultimate need for security could be found outside of Christ. Martin was looking to Sara to meet his needs, and when she obviously began to fail to meet them, instead of accepting that she could never meet his deepest longings, he 'punished' her by withdrawing from her, and took up the offer of a short-term solution. Sara depended on Martin to meet her needs, and when he failed her, she initially 'punished' him by withdrawing, and continued to 'punish' him for the sense of betrayal that she felt.

Martin and Sara are now in their mid-thirties, are still married to each other, and would describe their love for each other as infinitely stronger that it was over ten years ago. Although the road back from the abyss was not easy, and took some years to travel, they succeeded. Somebody asked them if they were committed to being the best people that God wanted them to be. Somewhere beneath the pain and frustration was a strong Christian commitment, and with help they learned to show each other unconditional love. They started demonstrating love to each other in mundane, practical ways, regardless of feelings, as an act of obedience to Christ. When that love was rejected or misunderstood (as it often was in the early stages), they learned not to withdraw and stop loving (as they had done previously), but to remind themselves that they were loved by Christ and were acting to please him. Although they legitimately wanted each other's love, and as a married couple had a right to expect it, they didn't *need* it in order to feel secure.

Such an account looks trite in print, and cannot do justice to the complexity of the issues or the pain and difficulty of the reality, but both Sara and Martin can testify to the freedom they found to give love again from a position of security in God.

Wants and needs

There are enormous differences between 'wants' and 'needs', and at the heart of our frustrations lies a failure to think biblically. We confuse wants with needs and tell ourselves that we must achieve certain goals. We convince ourselves that we need to, when we don't actually need to. Or we try to look for someone or something to meet our ultimate needs outside of Christ.

Peter's multiple sclerosis has left him with several legitimate wants. It is natural for him to want health, work, love, sexual fulfilment, and a family. God, who made him, designed a body and personality that would want these things. In helping Peter we have to take account of the pain that he feels because of these unfulfilled wants. Because we are human, with many similar wants, we can begin to understand what he feels. He has grown up, however, in a society which has convinced him that his wants are needs, and that he needs these things to be valuable and loved. But only Christ can meet those ultimate needs. The only hope of growth for Peter is to accept that many of his wants will probably remain unsatisfied, but that Christ can meet his deepest longings. We don't write this tritely. Peter's pain is real; but we believe that it is possible, even for Peter, to find peace, resting under the shadow of 'his wings'.

Mary's desire for some measure of independence and satisfaction in being able to do things is understandable and legitimate. So is Richard's desire for job satisfaction and a chance to enjoy the good things of life. God made us creative beings with an ability to think and plan. He saw that his creation was good, and we shouldn't be afraid of taking legitimate pleasure in being part of God's world. One of Jesus' first miracles was to help out at a wedding celebration where the hosts had run out of wine! And we can understand Sara and Michael wanting human love and being hurt. It is quite natural for us to want to travel down the road of achieving these goals. When the 'wants' road becomes blocked, however, the only way of avoiding the frustrating experience of continually crashing into the barrier is to let Jesus put the importance of the 'wants' road into perspective.

The only thing that we actually *need* in all eternity is a relationship with Jesus Christ.

chapter four

Wishing your life away

He drove into the parking space with the newly painted name hardly dry. It was a new, bright, white Mercedes estate, immaculately clean and sparkling. When I had studied the job advertisement I saw that the salary being offered was £10,000 a year more than I was earning. I felt that I could do the job, and I could certainly use the money to help ease some of the present financial pressure and make life more comfortable for the family. He got the job, and I coveted his parking space, his new status, his car, and his salary.

When looking at what I might legitimately have, I saw a slight possibility that I could have it, and that slight possibility led me to being obsessed with getting it. I lost sight of what I already had. It became second-rate and trivial. I became discontented, and when I couldn't get what I wanted, I started to feel betrayed and bitter. Like an immature child, I felt that I had the right to have everything I wanted, and that only a mean parent would deny me it. It ate into me for some time.

If that feeling of frustration had been allowed to develop indefinitely, it could have led into further sin. I could have become so frustrated that I might have started to want to destroy the other person, using a variety of subtle techniques. I could have criticized his work behind his back. I could have resisted any changes he wanted to bring in. I could have frozen him out of any relationship with me. I could have 'fought' him on every available occasion in order to attempt to destroy his enjoyment of what he had, just because I couldn't have it. It would be like repeatedly driving a car against an enormous barrier blocking the road in a futile attempt to knock it out of the way.

It is very uncomfortable to realize that our thought-life can include covetousness. It is an ugly word for something that somes naturally, often unbidden, and does not appear to do anyone any harm – hardly a sin at all, really! Or is it?

It is very uncomfortable to remember that God condemns covetousness in his ten rules for healthy living.

> You must not be envious of your neighbour's
> house, or want to sleep with his wife, or want to
> own his slaves, oxen, donkeys, or anything else
> he has (Exodus 20:17, Living Bible).

Thinking a little about what you fancy doesn't do you good

The Bible makes it clear that we must not covet any possessions, livestock, or any person already spoken for who belongs to another person's household. So if we wish that something or someone we have no right to could be ours, we are coveting. Obviously we experience frustration because our thoughts are fixed on what simply cannot be. Oh, if only we were not Christians, not tithing, had morals like the world . . .!

It does look shocking put into print. But many of us *do* indulge in a bit of quiet coveting, very discreetly, so that we hardly notice it ourselves – don't we? We have experienced a general dissatisfaction with things, a sense of missing something that might have been and probably should have been. But of course, it can't be, so we sigh and push our frustration aside in order to get on with good old, boring old daily (Christian) life. Unfortunately, the same spiritual laws apply to this situation as to any other: an unconfessed, unacknowledged sin spoils our relationship with God. It also has a knock-on effect on other relationships; you may slyly kick the cat, if you have one. Other people besides you get frustrated. The frustration caused by someone's envy or covetousness is a block, just like that caused by any other circumstance.

Jesus makes it plain in his teaching that covetous thoughts lead to sinful deeds.

You have heard that it was said, 'Do not commit adultery.' But I tell you that anyone who looks at a woman lustfully has already committed adultery with her in his heart (Matthew 5:27–28).

His brother James wrote on a similar theme:

> . . . each one is tempted when, by his own evil desire, he is dragged away and enticed. Then, after desire has conceived, it gives birth to sin; and sin, when it is full-grown, gives birth to death (James 1:14–15).

This is strong stuff, uncompromising, and meant to open our eyes to the consequences of an unruly thought-life. Covetousness is more than just frustrating; it's dangerous as well.

A *long history*

It seems that one of the first sins in history was that of covetousness.

> When the woman saw the fruit of the tree was good for food and pleasing to the eye, *and also desirable for gaining wisdom*, she took some and ate it. She also gave some to her husband, who was with her, and he ate it (Genesis 3:6, our italics).

One could argue that the initial sin took place between verses 5 and 6 of Genesis 3, since the woman (and presumably the man, 'who was with her') doubted God's goodness, in response to the serpent's subtle suggestions. Both the man and the woman, however, certainly desired the fruit, which they had no right to have, and they followed the desire with the actions of taking and eating. The whole of the human race has been suffering from frustration ever since.

Joshua, leader of the Israelites after Moses, is another person who experiences intense distress as a result of another's covetousness. After the encouraging victory at Jericho, the next stage of the campaign is planned carefully: men are sent to spy out the land around the town of Ai. They return with some advice for Joshua.

> Not all the people will have to go up against
> Ai. Send two or three thousand men to take it
> and do not weary all the people, for only a few
> men are there (Joshua 7:3).

Joshua acts on their advice and sends 3,000 men, but they suffer a humiliating defeat in which thirty-six Israelites lose their lives. The effect on the nation is disastrous: 'the hearts of the people melted and became like water' (Joshua 7:5). Joshua himself spends the entire day face down on the ground in front of the ark of the covenant, and when he does address God he more or less says it's all over.

Ah, Sovereign LORD, why did you ever bring
this people across the Jordan to deliver us into
the hands of the Amorites to destroy us? If only
we had been content to stay on the other side of
the Jordan! O Lord, what can I say, now that
Israel has been routed by its enemies? The
Canaanites and the other people of the country
will hear about this and they will surround us
and wipe out our name from the earth. What
then will you do for your own great name?
(Joshua 7:7–9).

Joshua is way beyond frustration; he is in despair, and
although he is ready to repent of whatever it is that has
brought this disaster on them all, he doesn't have a clue
what it is. God tells him that 'Israel has sinned' (Joshua
7:11). All the silver, gold, bronze and iron found in
Jericho were 'devoted things', that is, they were given
over to the Lord and were to be stored in the treasury of
the Lord's house. But someone had taken from Jericho
some items that he had no right to, and put them with
his own possessions (see Joshua 6:24 and 7:11). God
gives Joshua the responsibility of finding out who had
done this thing.

Joshua begins this unpleasant but necessary task early
the next morning. It turns out to be a man called Achan,
who confesses (when it becomes obvious that he is the
guilty one). He describes the crime he committed:

When I saw in the plunder a beautiful robe
from Babylonia, two hundred shekels of silver

and a wedge of gold weighing fifty shekels, I
coveted them and took them. They are hidden
in the ground inside my tent, with the silver
underneath (Joshua 7:21).

One man's covetousness led to all kinds of pain and
frustration for other people. Thirty-six families were left
without a human provider; several children were left
without a father; several women faced a future without
the man they had loved.

There are many other instances of covetousness in the
Bible. In the Old Testament, for example, David covets
Uriah's beautiful wife (2 Samuel 11:1–3); Amnon covets
his half-sister Tamar and makes himself ill with
frustration (2 Samuel 13:1–2); and Absalom covets his
father's job (2 Samuel 15:4–6). In the New Testament,
Ananias and Sapphira covet recognition and status
among the believers (Acts 5:1–10); and a sorcerer
named Simon becomes a Christian, but covets power
and is rebuked by Peter (Acts 8:9–24). In each case, the
frustration that goes hand in glove with covetousness
and envy leads to sinful actions, just as the apostle James
outlines in his letter. In several of the cases above, it
literally led to death for at least one person.

The beguiling short-cut

When you covet, the possession or person seems
beautiful, wonderful and desirable. It probably *is* all
those things. But why is it not so wonderful once you

have achieved your heart's desire? Jacob succeeded in obtaining the blessing from Esau, but as a result lost almost everything else and had to make his own way in the world. His covetousness became a curse on the whole family. If we are honest, many of us have dreamed of owning something rather special from time to time. Some of us have gone on to see the dream come true. Strangely, though, sometimes the reality of ownership is not quite as satisfying as we had imagined. Why is this so? One reason might be that the 'something rather special' has become our heart's desire. While that was happening, the desired object begins to appear so wonderful that it is as if it casts a glow over the rest of our life. It's as if we pretend (or believe) that many other things in our life will be wonderful too, 'if only . . .'

Imagine a day one weekend when our children (James and Nina's) are bored and tetchy. We are bored and tetchy too, and long for a break from the children's bickering. There are days when they seem to actually enjoy it, in a perverse kind of way, but we never do. The solution might be to all pile into the car and go out somewhere. Somewhere over the rainbow there is a place where children are sweet and loving towards each other. We hope that it might be in a nearby adventure playground. So we fix our hopes on that and start to get ready.

The arguments continue in the bathroom, in the bedrooms, down the stairs and all the way to the car. But we fix our hope on the adventure playground and the wide open spaces around it. The children continue to bicker. We snap at them and then alienate them by dragging in all the things they did that annoyed us in the last three days. We get tight-lipped with each other. If only we were at the playground now! Things will be different there. We shall sit on a bench and hold hands while the darlings play happily and *leave us in peace*.

When we arrive, the children burst out of the car and disappear towards the swings, climbing frame and fort. They play, meet friends, and have a wonderful time. Meanwhile we, having got what we wanted, are unable to enjoy it because we are feeling upset, and cross with the children and with each other. We feel guilty for being bad parents and guilty for wishing that parenting was not a full-time occupation. We have got our heart's desire, but the glow that it was meant to cast has turned to a dingy blue. We had been full of 'if only' in our hearts, forgetting that the solution to our problems (peaceful family relationships) was, at this point, a little more complex than our short-cut (get the children out of our hair).

You could argue that, in the illustration above, we were not coveting anything wrong. But we were not quite right towards each other and our children either. We had become so taken with the idea of what we wanted that we had ignored, on the way, principles of justice, forgiveness and love towards family members. Our short-cut did not work out in the way we wanted. When people covet things, they are sometimes looking for a short-cut, a quick and easy way out of some of life's difficulties. Then when they obtain their heart's desire, the glow disappears.

The difference between the good and the best

Covetousness can be harmful, but in fact it is harmful *not* to be covetous of the best that God wants to give us. Sometimes we set our earthly expectations low, in order to avoid disappointment. The danger comes when this kind of outlook spills over into expectations of what Christian life should be. It is good to avoid sin, but it is hard to survive without anything positive and true to take its place. Low expectations of God, and of ourselves as his children, lead to frustration and a rather hollow Christian life. The good news is that God wants us to set our hearts on something after all.

> Since, then, you have been raised with Christ,
> set your hearts on things above, where Christ is
> seated at the right hand of God. Set your minds
> on things above, not on earthly things. For you
> died, and your life is now hidden with Christ in
> God. When Christ, who is your life, appears,
> then you also will appear with him in glory
> (Colossians 3:1–4).

God says that there are some things that it is OK to covet.

Strangely enough, if we follow this advice, and set our hearts and minds on 'things above', then a real and positive glow is cast over the rest of our life. The mechanism that works to our ruin when we covet earthly things works for our benefit when we covet heavenly things – those 'good and perfect gifts' that we read about in James 1:17. Why is this? Why does it work this way? It must be because the heavenly things are real, solid and of lasting (eternal) value.

In the run-up to Christmas (any time from January onwards!), when television commercials encourage us to buy our loved ones everything from monsters with uncontrollable hair and questionable parentage, to handy finger-shredders for the kitchen, certain very expensive items are presented as 'timeless'. The tone of such a commercial is a world away from the trashy and flashy. Instead, it is cool, elegant, sophisticated, altogether on a higher plane. It is quite laughable when you realize that this is only another advertisement for something that will eventually wear out, need repairing or go out of fashion. The things that God values, however, really are timeless and lasting.

When I die, I shall leave behind me every single thing I ever owned. I shall take with me only myself and the timeless things God has given me: my life in Christ (Colossians 3:3) and my 'clothes'. These may include compassion, kindness, humility, gentleness and patience; forgiveness like God's forgiveness; and love as both a covering and a binding (Colossians 3:12–14). If I have set my heart on these things, perhaps I shall leave this life with at least some clothing, even if it is a bit thin, patched, torn or holey in places. In fact, if I have cooperated with God in what *he* desires for me, these clothes will not be things that can be taken off and put on again, because they will be part of me.

The frustration of coveting heavenly things and not getting them is not necessarily a bad thing. But if only that quality of patience would hurry up and arrive *today*! Yesterday I was so angry at myself for my lack of gentleness I slammed my fist into the door. And I really would have compassion on people if only they were not so stupid as to bring trouble on themselves! It is an uncomfortable and frustrating fact that heavenly things seem to take time and effort to acquire.

A *conscious turning*

It would be good to know how to use our frustration over our spiritual progress positively. The first thing to do is to prepare our hearts. Even if we are committed Christians, this may take some time. In reality we have died to earthly things (Colossians 3:2), and we have a resurrection life in Jesus now (Colossians 3:1). Our citizenship is in heaven (Philippians 3:20). We are even 'seated . . . with him in the heavenly realms in Christ Jesus' (Ephesians 2:6). But perhaps we have drifted away from that reality so that 'real life' and our 'spiritual life' are at odds with each other in some respects (and they must be, if we keep them in separate compartments). It is important to acknowledge this before God and to take the further step of giving up to him those other things we are secretly coveting. If the desires of our hearts are not really for heavenly things, we need to tell him about it. We need to ask him to turn our eyes (inward and outward) to his truth. Paul writes about the eyes of our hearts:

> I pray . . . that the eyes of your heart may be
> enlightened in order that you may know the
> hope to which he has called you, the riches of
> his glorious inheritance in the saints, and his
> incomparably great power for us who believe.
> That power is like the working of his mighty
> strength, which he exerted in Christ when he
> raised him from the dead and seated him at his
> right hand in the heavenly realms, far above all
> rule and authority, power and dominion, and
> every title that can be given, not only in the
> present age but also in the one to come
> (Ephesians 1:18–21).

When the eyes of our heart are enlightened, we begin to be excited by every good and perfect gift that God has for us. The enlightening of the eyes of our hearts is part of a continual preparation that we can engage in, in our spiritual development.

A friend of ours recently started his renewal with this prayer that he wrote in his journal and shared with us. If appropriate, you might like to adapt it and use it yourself.

> Father, what have I become? Someone twisted
> and aching inside because I couldn't get what I
> wanted. You know how I felt undervalued and
> under-used at church. I wanted to use the gifts
> you have given me, but couldn't. Nobody asked
> me. Nobody saw any real worth in me. Nobody
> wanted to know. And because of that there was

all that anger, all that grief, all that depression – the sulking, the shouting, the immaturity. I am ashamed to think of how my family suffered. I wanted something so badly that I lost sight of what was important and I started to wander away from you. I coveted a role, a recognition, a purpose, that you have said I am not to have at this time. Father, forgive that destructive covetousness. Please build in me a stronger desire to know you more and to trust you in the darkness . . .

Here are some further practical suggestions for dealing with covetousness.

Stop denying the reality of God's goodness

When we covet, we are tempted to think that God doesn't love us as much as he should because he has given other people good things that we want. If God really loved me, we argue, he would have given me the same gifts and money that he has given other 'successful' Christians. In our more rational moments, however, we know that our parents' distribution of their wealth is not necessarily an indication of their love. Children may have different needs and be at different stages of development. It may not be wise to give your seven-year-old son the same amount of pocket money as your sixteen-year-old daughter. God is sovereign, and doesn't have to give anything. We need to learn to value what God, in his goodness, has given, and not allow what we haven't got to destroy the enjoyment of what we have.

Accept that you have a training need

Paul writes:

> I have learned to be content whatever the circumstances. I know what it is to be in need, and I know what it is to have plenty. I have learned the secret of being content in any and every situation, whether well fed or hungry, whether living in plenty or in want. I can do everything through him who gives me strength (Philippians 4:11–13).

Paul faced many temptations to frustration (see below), and he is admitting that his contentment wasn't automatic or easy. It was something he learned. He had to practise thinking through the issues. There would be times when he failed and lapsed into discontentment and frustration. But there is hope. He was able to do everything through Christ's help, and Jesus helped him in the difficult learning process. We shall need to practise taking hold of our thinking patterns and redirecting them along biblical paths. We may not be able to find the meaning behind everything that blocks our way, but we can be sure about God's desire to give us the best in Christ, and of his compassion for us. In heaven, we shall not get everything that we want, but we shall know that what God wanted for us was perfect.

Develop a new passion

Although we are saved once and for all when we commit our lives to the Lord Jesus Christ, it requires more than a single decision to set our hearts and minds on our inheritance in him. It is almost too obvious to mention that there are very varied opportunities to set our minds and hearts on earthly goods or earthly goals. But heavenly things can quickly become rather remote, unreachable and even unreal to us. The demands of everyday life (that useful scapegoat) can somehow discourage us from bothering very much about reading the Bible and spending time alone with God.

We (James and Nina) have tried everything from an hour with the Authorized Version before breakfast every day (that was a long time ago!) to ignoring *that book* for weeks – let's be honest, for months on end. We have had all sorts of variations and all sorts of reasons and excuses for changing our methods (not all of them bad ones). But the only thing that really contributes to changing our desires is a dip, a dive, or better still, a long swim and a float (time to reflect) in the Bible, to let God's Word inform and instruct our hearts and minds. Obviously, the more regularly one takes this exercise, the more readily one deals with frustration and begins to make some progress. Counter covetousness by cultivating the contemplation of God as revealed in his Word.

We won't rid ourselves of any covetousness by saying: 'I must get rid of this covetousness.' We need to confess our sin, draw close to God, and then move forward in his work. If we are frustrated because we are coveting something that God is saying no to, either temporarily or permanently, then we need to redirect our heart's desire. After twenty-one years of marriage, we have learned to counter the attractive pull of intimacy outside the marriage by consciously fostering intimacy within the marriage. Here are three guidelines to help foster what is best, rather than what appears attractive for a moment.

1. Quality of time spent together is more important than quantity of time. When we were first married we had plenty of time to ourselves. Changing life demands, and the arrival of children, meant that the amount has changed. We have to work at the quality. If one of us is away, a phone call is better than no contact at all. Fifteen minutes of quality time with God each day is better than thirty minutes of self-righteous pride or guilt and daydreaming. Choose a time that is best for you. Ask someone you respect to help you get more from your Bible study.

2. Openness and honesty prevent hardness and coldness. We need to be open with God, confessing sin regularly, depending on him for all things, and delighting in his goodness. Consider keeping a journal to record your thoughts, feelings, and spiritual longings. We've also found the discipline of regular worship to be helpful. It's hard to hide things that need to be confessed and worship at the same time. Worship can help honesty and inspire love.

3. Planning, not circumstances, should determine our meetings. Saying no to somebody or something means that we are able to prioritize on what is important. It is a constant reminder to both of us that the relationship is

important. If we are to fall in love with God again so that our hearts are not set on earthly things, we need to create space and time for the relationship. Dare to turn the television off in order to meet God.

Covetousness is a sign that we have lost our first love. We need to consciously work to rekindle that love. A new passion for Jesus will help guard our hearts and minds.

Set new priorities

There were clearly many occasions when Paul must have been tempted to covet the relatively simple, secure, affluent lifestyle he could have had as a Jewish scholar and teacher. Just think of the closing chapters in Acts as he made his journey to Rome: threats against his life, shipwreck, and finally imprisonment. These circumstances and privations would have been frustrating for anybody. Paul, however, had a new priority. His top priority was no longer to make a comfortable life for himself, but to preach the gospel. Material inconveniences took on a new perspective. When he was shipwrecked he didn't rail against God, but accepted the God-given opportunity to minister to other people. When in prison and unable to preach to large groups, he witnessed to the guards and wrote letters to the churches.

There are many occasions when it would be understandable if we wanted to change our circumstances. But until God allows those circumstances to change, we have to get on with the work of the kingdom. Coveting a different life will just lead to inactivity, self-pity, and depression.

Last Sunday morning our family trooped back to a car that had been sitting in the sun for over two hours. It was stifling inside. We encouraged the children to 'belt up' quickly so that we could set off and get air moving through the car. There's a sense in which we become what we do. As we start to get moving again in the kingdom of God, as we start to know our heart's beating in tune with God's heart, then he draws near to us, and the Spirit starts to flow through us to other people.

chapter five

I can't wait

I must do something

When you're frustrated, there are times when you feel that you've just got to do something. You can't merely sit back and wait. You want to pick up a phone and 'sort something out', or get in the car and go to somebody straight away and tell him what you think. Perhaps you want to make an appointment immediately so that others (including God) understand in no uncertain terms that you definitely want progress on a particular issue. 'I want you to know that I'm *not* going to accept what has happened or take it lying down, and my action of coming to talk to you now is signalling my determination to fight this thing.'

That quality of determination can be really useful at times. An acquaintance of ours, who is a senior manager in a large institution, has a well-developed 'terrier' quality. If she decides to do something, she will tirelessly work to achieve that goal and will accept defeat only reluctantly. She seems to be someone who really believes in the saying that a successful manager never sees problems, only opportunities for change. If thwarted in her work goals, she will immediately make phone calls, visit people, write memoranda, and forcefully lobby people to change their views or remove barriers to her achievement. She would probably admit, however, that left unchecked, such a 'terrier quality' can easily degenerate into impatient bullying.

Although there are times when we don't want to wait, the Bible puts a high premium on being patient.

What is patience?

Have you ever pretended to be patient? Perhaps the partner you were courting kept you waiting, or a colleague delayed the start of a meeting. You may have smiled and told that person that it didn't matter, while you prided yourself on your calm exterior. But what about the panic as you waited for the partner to arrive, or the explosion behind your colleague's back? Patience is more than a respectable pretence at placidity.

Neither is patience just blind resignation to unavoidable facts. During a tragedy, some are able to adopt a fatalistic acceptance that whatever will be, will be. But the acceptance is made in defeat, rather than in hope.

The patience that God wants to build in us must be more dynamic than resignation to the inevitable. It must be authenticated by true peace and not simply a socially acceptable façade. The patience that God wants to build can't be dependent on a particular temperament. Such a patience is doomed to failure, and it would mean that vast numbers of Christians could have no hope of breaking free from their frustration. The Bible points to a patience based on quiet confidence in God. James writes: 'See how the farmer waits for the land to yield its valuable crop and how patient he is for the autumn and spring rains. You too, be patient and stand firm, because the Lord's coming is near' (James 5:7–8).

The source of patience lies not in our temperament, stoicism, or social etiquette, but in our concept of God and in our faith in him. If I am to control my frustration and impatience I need to understand my own limitations; a farmer can't make rain or give growth. I need to understand that I can rely on God to act in the most wise and merciful way, at the right time; the harvest will come. Also, I must consciously submit to his sovereignty. True patience is a calm endurance based on a certain knowledge that God is in control.

Why be patient?

Many of us wouldn't put impatience high on the list of character weaknesses that need to be dealt with. It is one of those things that we might get round to when we have the time. Being consumed with passion for somebody else's marriage partner or envious of next door's car is clearly a big problem, but we tend to regard impatience as a mere peccadillo. We need, however, to start taking impatience more seriously.

The apostle Paul, who during the course of his ministry had to deal with more than his fair share of difficult individuals and churches, commanded the Ephesians to 'be patient, bearing with one another in love' (Ephesians 4:2). Again, when giving advice to Christians about how to deal with potentially frustrating people (the idle, the timid, the weak), Paul urged them to 'be patient with everyone' (1 Thessalonians 5:14).

God not only commands patience, he also compels it by his example. We often struggle to be patient with individuals; he shows great forbearance to nations and to the world, as well as to his imperfect disciples.

If it had been left to us, we would probably have given up on Abraham. Just imagine him being considered as a candidate for church leadership! What a field day his critics would have had – too pragmatic, too immoral, too rude! When the promised son didn't appear, Abraham took the matter into his own hands, and the descendants of Ishmael, the resulting child of his wife's servant, would perpetually live in hostility towards their neighbours. If this wasn't bad enough, Abraham twice tried to pretend that his wife was only his sister while they were living in another country. This brought disease and barrenness on the rulers who had acted as hosts. Then when Abraham begged God to spare Sodom, he had the boldness to argue and change the conditions five times. Yet God remained faithful to his promise to make his imperfect servant into a great nation.

When dealing with difficult groups, Jesus showed

that love is patient. In spite of constant personal pressure and suffering, Jesus continually gave to his disciples, though they were argumentative and slow to understand, and would ultimately desert him during his own most painful experience. When dealing with the whole world, God delays judgment and endures our rebellion. As Peter explained: 'The Lord is not slow in keeping his promise, as some understand slowness. He is patient with you, not wanting anyone to perish, but everyone to come to repentance' (2 Peter 3:9). Patience is a key characteristic of God, and we must grow in patience if we want to reflect his image.

A powerful cocktail

Frustration and impatience often go hand in hand. They feed off each other and rapidly help each other grow out of all proportion. Once that key sense of proportion is lost, rational and spiritual judgment becomes impaired. 'I don't care what you think, or what the Bible says, this issue has become very important to me. It's consuming me. I've lost my anchor. I'm being tossed about. I must do something.' When you add the inevitable flow of strong emotion and the fear of not being able to control the future, you have a powerful cocktail.

In their impatience, Gary and Rebekah rushed into a marriage that, to concerned onlookers, seemed a very unsuitable relationship. She was so afraid that she would end up unable to find a Christian man that she took the first one who became available in five years. He was equally desperate to get married, to assert his independence, and to find a replacement for his mother. Both of them threw their better judgment out of the window. Impatience also throws light on why they rushed out of the marriage three years later.

In his impatience, Nick decided to leave the church after storming out of a meeting with the elders. God had told him that the church needed to start that particular ministry now. When the elders initially expressed reservations about the wisdom of doing *exactly* what he wanted, and *to his timescale*, impatience led him to reject biblical teaching on submission and guidance and go into a spiritual wilderness for several years.

In its impatience, the congregation in Little Puddletown appointed a pastor. Their previous pastor had been so wonderful; they missed him so much. Three years of visiting preachers made them ache for consistency and pastoral care. They were frustrated and impatient for God to answer their prayers. Geoffrey seemed to be the answer. They appointed him in haste without trying to make an objective assessment of either their expectations or his. After six months they all realized that there was a serious mismatch; the decision taken in haste wasn't going to work out. He left three years later.

Impulsive words can kill growing friendships, and when we are impatient with people, we break social bonds. We may want to win people for Christ or build God's word in them, but if we are impatient, we destroy the effectiveness of what we are trying to do. However much we may apologize afterwards, it is often difficult to rebuild credibility with people who do not have

God's ability to forget what God has forgiven. We give people a reason for not taking us seriously. Patience is part of the oil that keeps the communication machine functioning smoothly.

However attractive impatience may seem at the time, as a way out of a frustrating situation, it unfortunately makes matters worse. When a brick wall appears on our path, it may be tempting to reverse the car for a few hundred yards and then slam down the accelerator and hurtle towards the obstacle at 100 mph. But often all that happens is that, although the wall may appear to shift a few inches, we wreck the car and end up in the accident and emergency department with our unfortunate passengers.

One of the saddest stories in the Old Testament highlights the contrast in attitude between impatience and patience. David had a son, Absalom, who couldn't wait. This impatience caused a series of events which eventually led to great suffering for others (including his father) and to Absalom's own death.

It is difficult to say where the story begins. In one sense it begins with David's immorality with Bathsheba (2 Samuel 11), because the events fulfil the prophecy made by Nathan: judgment would fall on David's household because David had despised God. Nathan tells him in 2 Samuel 12:9–14 that

- the sword shall never depart from his house;
- his own wives will be raped in public by someone close to him;
- Bathsheba's child would die.

There is a real sense in which David suffers the consequences of an impatient son because of his own impatient actions with Bathsheba.

In a more obvious sense the story begins when David's son Amnon rapes his own sister, Tamar (2 Samuel 13). The other brother, Absalom, is justifiably outraged on his sister's behalf, and daily sees some of the consequences of the rape, since the desolate Tamar moves in to Absalom's house. David too is outraged, but fails to punish Amnon. We can only guess as to possible reasons. Perhaps, like many fathers, he was reluctant to take serious action against his own children; perhaps he didn't know what to do; perhaps he felt morally unable to act because of his own sexual sin with Bathsheba and his murder of Uriah. In the event, nothing seems to have been done.

Although Absalom may have started with a just cause, he quickly loses the moral ground when, two years later, he contrives to have Amnon murdered (2 Samuel 13:23–35). Traditional channels of justice through the king have failed Absalom, and he cannot wait for God to avenge evil. Absalom is impatient for revenge.

For three years, Absalom stays out of the way in Geshur. David's servants notice the king constantly mourning for Absalom, and they contrive to get David to allow Absalom to return to Jerusalem. David agrees to this, although he doesn't allow Absalom to see him. Absalom accepts the situation for two years, but when David doesn't soften in the way that Absalom desires, he sends for Joab, one of the king's advisers. Joab refuses to visit. Although Absalom may have started with a legitimate expectation that one of David's advisers would visit David's son, he unlawfully burns Joab's field in order to get Joab to see him (2 Samuel 14:28–33). So Absalom gets his own way, not only in engineering an audience with Joab, but also in being reconciled to the king. He feels that he has done no wrong and cannot wait to be vindicated.

The remainder of the story follows the pattern of impatient bullying and manoeuvring. Many of the things he wants are understandable and legitimate, but he cannot wait and trust. He has to achieve certain things, and has to achieve them according to his timetable. He would seem to be a very insecure man. David is slow to give Absalom a recognized position, and so he manipulates people in order to steal the hearts of many (2 Samuel 15:1–5). With Amnon dead, Absalom may have legitimately expected to inherit the throne, but he cannot wait for power and he plots a rebellion, forcing David to flee Jerusalem (2 Samuel 15 – 18). Absalom is finally killed by an accident on the battlefield. His head is caught in a tree, and he is later attacked by David's troops. Presumably he is forcefully reminded, before he dies, that impatient bullies cannot always get their own way!

David, on the other hand, had learned that God, rather than he himself, was the only ultimate source of power, strength, and protection: 'You are a shield around me, O LORD . . . the LORD sustains me . . . From the LORD comes deliverance . . .' (Psalm 3:3, 5, 8).

Patience really is a virtue and, like all virtues, it needs

to be cultivated. Sometimes we try to excuse our impatience as part of our character. 'That's the way I am. I've always been like that. I can't help it. You'll just have to accept that part of me.' But because God is constantly challenging and enabling us to become more like Jesus, we need to take responsibility for our own sin and seek God's help in producing this particular fruit of the Spirit. Patience may be a virtue, but with God we can and should become virtuous people.

How can I become more patient?

Many of us recognize our impatience and the damage it has caused or is causing. For some of us, impatience has become the all too familiar first response to frustrating events and circumstances that block our path. But recognizing impatience, and even feeling guilty about it, is not the same as trying to overcome it. What we want to do in the remainder of this chapter is to share some of the strategies we are finding helpful in dealing with our own impatience.

One of the first things we need to do when tempted to be impatient is to consciously affirm our faith in God, and that means affirming our faith in the parts of his character that we are tempted to doubt.

In the Sermon on the Mount, Jesus warns his disciples that they are not to be like the pagans in their behaviour. Ultimately all behaviour stems from a set of beliefs. When we behave like unbelievers in our impatience, it is because there are times when we believe the same things as they do about God. Behind our impatient actions is an un-Christian set of implicit assumptions: 'I can't be sure that God knows what he is doing. I doubt his perfect knowledge, his perfect goodness, his perfect timing, his perfect power. I must feel that I am in control of everything all the time.'

We need to combat this kind of thinking in a positive and godly way.

Have you ever been on a mystery bus tour? A friend of ours was recently taken on a mystery tour for the day by some church members as a birthday present. Just imagine it was you: someone arrives at your front door early in the morning, says you are going out for the day (but won't tell you where), and takes you off to the minibus. You are naturally surprised and curious. A slight degree of unease and disorientation would be understandable. You would, however, probably end up enjoying the day, having had something like the following conversation with yourself: 'I trust and love these people. They have my best interests at heart. They are not perfect, but they have planned this journey. I don't know what time we shall get back, but I'm sure they have a timescale. They know what they are doing. They may take me where I wouldn't have chosen for myself, but I know they love me. I desperately want to know the route and destination, but I have to accept that they will tell me only when they wish to. I have to accept that this is their bus and their plans; they are in control. We are going on a journey, and this time I am not driving. I don't feel entirely comfortable, but I'm going to accept it.'

If you didn't have something like the above conversation where you asserted your faith in your friends, you would not enjoy the trip. You would miss the beauty of the journey by constantly fretting about the destination and timescale. The faithfulness of your friends would be tested to the limits as you argued with the bus-driver, trying to bully her with your constant refrain of: 'But I want to go this way! I want to go this way! . . .' As God's people, let's not treat God like that. He is, after all, perfect, trustworthy and wise.

Abraham exercised faith

We have used the example of Abraham to illustrate the dangers of impatience. Towards the end of his life, however, he had clearly learned how to exercise faith in the face of trying circumstances, so avoiding hasty actions and disastrous consequences. He did father a child through Hagar because he couldn't wait for God's promise to be fulfilled, and he did lie about his relationship to Sarah, but on Mount Moriah he stood firm.

When God asked Abraham to sacrifice his son Isaac, it was not only painful for Abraham (and presumably for Isaac!), but also extremely frustrating as well. The request seemed to represent a huge barrier on the path to personal progress for Abraham and Isaac, and to spiritual progress for the extremely young Jewish nation. Impatient Abraham would have attempted to run from God (like Jonah), or taken an unacceptable substitute (as with Hagar). But the patient Abraham obeyed God. We can only guess what Abraham must have been thinking as he travelled with Isaac to Mount Moriah, but it seems reasonable to infer that he reminded himself about God's faithfulness in provision, his mercy and compassion, his repeated promises, and his ability to miraculously intervene and control events in time; so that by the time of the sacrifice, Abraham's faith enabled him to carry out his Father's wish. He overcame the temptation to act hastily and impulsively by exercising faith.

We do not receive a pay-off from faith by passively waiting to feel good. Having a piece of paper called a cheque should guarantee that we get the money, but we need to actively cash what we hold. This is what Abraham did on the way up Mount Moriah; it is a good example to follow.

Acknowledging who is in control

It is much easier to be patient when we feel we have at least some control over events. Circumstances may be difficult, but if we can guide things along, we should be able to get them back on course in due time. It is very hard – even scary – when we feel we have little or no control. How can we be patient then?

The easy answer, as every Christian knows, is that God is in control. We all confess that 'Jesus is Lord', and pray, 'Your kingdom come.' Strange, then, that we so easily forget this and act as if we believed that 'I am in control. I am lord of my life. I have a master plan which I have every right to follow.' Of course, we say these things to ourselves much more subtly than that, and in a very secretive way. In spite of our Christian confession, we still behave as if our right to control our own lives were a given. The most subtle form of this is the assumption that God's plans and ours neatly coincide. It is a form of pride which the New Testament goes so far as to call evil.

> Now listen, you who say, 'Today or tomorrow
> we will go to this or that city, spend a year
> there, carry on business and make money.'
> Why, you do not even know what will happen
> tomorrow. What is your life? You are a mist
> that appears for a little while and then vanishes.
> Instead, you ought to say, 'If it is the Lord's
> will, we will live and do this or that.' As it is,
> you boast and brag. All such boasting is evil
> (James 4:13–16).

James is writing about inner attitude here. He says it is evil to have the attitude that we can plan our lives without reference to God. Making plans is perfectly all right, but in doing so, we must have God – our relationship to God – as our starting-point.

Jesus teaches us about the same issue (see, for example, Luke 14:25–34). He commends making plans and assessing situations carefully. Then he clearly states that a disciple has to give up 'everything'. This includes his imagined right to control his own life. The handing over of control, or submission to Christ's lordship, is one of the distinctives of a Christian, one of the things that makes us 'salty' (Luke 14:34).

Sadly, we easily forget to work out our commitment to these truths, and we get extremely impatient when God doesn't keep to 'his'/our schedule. When he is apparently oblivious to our plight, we want to overtly take control and 'make it happen'. We want to translate our frustration into action, but this is not necessarily what God wants at all.

The state of our house, at the time of writing, is potentially frustrating. After months of building work, where an existing room had been extended and new rooms added, we still have bare wires sticking out of the walls, no heating, no toilet in the new toilet, no shower in the shower . . . We could decide to have done with waiting and get on with it ourselves. As anyone who knows our DIY skills could tell you, however, the results would be disastrous and dangerous. So we exercise the wiser option of patience and wait for the people with the skills to arrive. We try to encourage our patience with the thought of God's sense of humour: that we should be writing a book about frustration while the house is in chaos for more than twice as long as we anticipated.

Just as we trust our builder (he is trustworthy, really) that he will see the whole project through to completion, we also trust God when he says that he is going to see his work in our lives through to completion (Philippians 1:6). It is not that God wants us to be passive, woodenly waiting to be wheeled down the right track. What he does long for is our glad and free cooperation with him in his good plans for us. '"For I know the plans I have for you," declares the LORD, "plans to prosper you and not harm you, plans to give you hope and a future"' (Jeremiah 29:11).

Cooperation with God can involve the challenge of facing potentially frustrating circumstances with patience and trust.

An interesting side-effect (or is it meant to be one of the main effects?) of the exercise of acknowledging God's control of our lives is that we learn to deal with other people in the way he deals with us. What we mean is this: God treats us with respect, not bullying or intimidating us, but patiently working for our good. In other words, in spite of his ultimate rights over us, he is not a heartless 'control freak'. As we experience this for ourselves, it gradually dawns on us that we are meant to deal with other people in the same way: with compassion and sensitivity, having their best interests at heart.

In her work, Amanda was becoming increasingly frustrated with a junior colleague who was regularly under-performing. The sad thing was that although Amanda was a Christian, she adopted the behaviour of her non-Christian peers, and joined in the aggressive, impatient remarks made to the under-performer. Amanda saw the situation as a threat to her control in the workplace. But once she understood more about God's over-all control, and decided to follow the pattern of cooperation, she was able to begin to face more calmly the legitimate concerns about poor performance, and deal more patiently and compassionately with her colleague.

chapter six

Relationships in a rut

They had worked beside each other in the church youth team for years. She had a husband and three children. He had no-one. Their adultery was at first exciting in its illicitness, and then it became crippling for both of them. They semi-accidentally spilled the beans one day, almost wanting to be caught. At the time of writing, she has not told her husband. Many people would encourage her not to do this. 'Why upset him needlessly,' they say, 'and risk him leaving her and disrupting the family life for the children?' She is content to listen to their advice. But in five years from now, what kind of person will she have become? Always on guard lest the truth slipped out. Always holding part of herself back from her husband. Never sharing everything with him. And how can she move forward in resolving issues in the relationship until both of them are honest about the problems? Our concern in this chapter is to argue that deceit and lies harm all relationships and lead to frustrating stagnation and further dishonesty.

There is something horribly persistent about a lie. Whether it is a 'whopper' of impressive dimensions ('Well, my dad has climbed every mountain in the world') or a slight but convenient alteration to the exact truth ('I was prevented from keeping our appointment due to unforeseen circumstances'), a lie persists in its effect, until it is put right. The lie that is forgotten or ignored colours a relationship with distrust.

The lie in the case study that follows had a pernicious effect on a whole family. Like any normal father, Jacob must have longed for his children to develop fully into mature people, able to relate well to each other, and to love and respect their parents. He must have hoped that any sibling jealousies would disappear over time, and that greater peace and harmony would descend on his family in his old age. The sons must have wanted to be able to successfully overcome the burdens of providing for a large family during years of famine, and have a life free from any additional burdens of emotional pain and guilt. Years after the original misdeeds, Jacob's family was paralysed by unconfessed sins that refused to lie down in the cupboard. It affected all their relationships and hindered their development as a loving unit.

Frustration and guilt

The background to the case study is well known. Seventeen-year-old Joseph was sold into slavery by his brothers, who lied to their father, Jacob, allowing him to believe that his favourite son had been killed by a wild animal.

The case study begins when Joseph is thirty-nine years old. His father, his brothers and their families are into the second year of a severe famine.

> When Jacob learned that there was grain in Egypt, he said to his sons, 'Why do you just keep looking at each other?' He continued, 'I have heard that there is grain in Egypt. Go down there and buy some for us, so that we may live and not die' (Genesis 42:1–2).

You can imagine crusty old Jacob sounding really exasperated. What was the matter with his sons? Why did Reuben and Judah look so stricken? Why were Dan and Naphtali exchanging guilty looks? Why were Gad and Asher hardly daring to meet each other's eyes, while Levi, Issachar and Zebulun tried to look nonchalant by sticking their thumbs in their belts? Perhaps Jacob tried again: 'Your wives and children are starving, you are all hungry and I am hardly able to keep body and soul together. *Go to Egypt and buy some grain!*'

> Then ten of Jacob's sons went down to buy grain from Egypt. But Jacob did not send Benjamin, Joseph's brother, with the others, because he was afraid that harm might come to him (Genesis 42:3–4).

It seems evident to us, from the story so far, that Jacob and his sons were stuck, emotionally and spiritually, at the day nineteen years earlier when Joseph 'went missing'.

The ten brothers who had conspired to sell Joseph into slavery had not stopped carrying the guilt for a single day. They had reasoned inwardly and with each other that, after all, they were not murderers; they had not killed him themselves. No, but the chances of a slave in Egypt still being alive after all this time were pretty thin. Worse still, they couldn't forget Joseph's cries. 'We saw how distressed he was when he pleaded with us for his life, but we would not listen' (Genesis 42:21). Then there had been the beginning of the deception of their father. What had seemed a neat way out at the time had just left a huge question about Joseph's fate hanging in the air.

Naturally, the brothers had worked hard at portraying honest and sincere grief over Joseph's demise, and then worked harder still at 'business as usual' and 'life must go on' through the best part of twenty years. They must have been thoroughly miserable inside. No wonder the mere mention of Egypt set the alarm bells ringing. Egypt was the very last place they wanted to think about, let alone visit!

Jacob, meanwhile, had never quite been able to believe in that 'honest grief' of his sons. Even in the midst of his own deep distress, it didn't look wholly believable. For one thing, there had been some fearsome family rows centred around Joseph. He may have been his father's favourite, but he certainly was not Reuben's or anyone else's. He could swear they looked guilty too. But then, bereaved relatives often did feel guilt. Jacob did himself: 'I should never have sent him after his brothers that day.' Did his sons feel similarly? 'We should have been able to do something. If only we had been there when the wild beasts attacked.' If so, Jacob wondered, why had that not faded away as the grieving process unfolded and healing began? But somehow, healing had never come for any of them. They all sensed it in themselves and each other; they were all frustrated by it. Yet no-one seemed able to do anything about it.

Jacob himself still had a sense of loss like a raw wound, and it tended to fester too, with dark suspicions that he suppressed. What *had* happened that day? His sons were an argumentative lot anyway, but Joseph had brought out the worst in them all with his foolish boasting. Well, nothing was ever going to happen to Benjamin. Little Benjamin would stay close to home, where his father could keep an eye on him. Perhaps, in time, Benjamin might grow up into a son almost as perfect as Joseph.

And think what life might have been like for poor Benjamin! Ever since he could remember, he may have been compared with his big brother. His self-esteem may have been very low. No-one seemed able to see him for who he was (if he was anybody): not his brothers, who avoided him as much as possible; nor his father, who saw him only through a 'Joseph filter'. Benjamin could almost have hated 'WonderBro'. What a wicked person he must be to want to hate his own dead brother!

It is easy to imagine how the whole family must have

been frustrated ('What *is* it about this family?') and unable to achieve healthy growth in their relationships. It was as if they all lived on a boat, with guilt at the prow, anger, fear and suspicion amidships, and unforgiveness in the stern. There was no escape.

There are families who are in the same boat as Jacob's. Issues are not confronted. Reconciliation is seen as impossible. 'Live and let live' tries to take its place, but is a poor substitute. Small remarks and allusions, veiled criticisms, teasing and 'jokes' at someone's expense, little meannesses, family get-togethers where people are either over-jolly or quietly withdrawn: these may bear witness to a frustrating situation. At least one person in the family is 'stuck' at some point in the past. There is a block around which no-one can move.

In this story, the 'impossible' happened. Joseph 'comes back from the dead', and the hidden skeletons start to come out of the family cupboard. When Joseph hears Judah pleading to take the punishment for the 'theft' in the place of Benjamin because of all that Jacob has already suffered, he breaks down and reveals his true identity. There is family shock, much weeping, and plenty of uncertainty about future relationships. But Joseph is compassionate. He tries to reassure them in their fear and doubts about his intentions, and, in forgiving them, breaks the power of the lie that had held the family in bondage for years.

But suppose Joseph had died in Egypt, so that the reconciliation recorded in Genesis 45 could not have happened. Could Jacob's family have removed the source of their frustration? We think they could have, with a lot of hard work, persistence, and God's help. We picture their action plans as looking something like this.

The ten sons

1. Tell Dad the truth about Joseph's disappearance.
2. Take responsibility individually for our own part in that day's events.
3. Name the wrong thoughts, words and actions involved.
4. Ask Dad's forgiveness personally.
5. Receive forgiveness from Dad.
6. Go through steps 1–5 with God.
7. Forgive other brothers (and Benjamin) and seek forgiveness from them.
8. Go through steps 1–5 with our own wives and children.

That would be a start, clearing the way for those ten men to experience growth, reality and openness in family relationships.

Jacob

1. Listen to what each of the ten said.
2. Forgive each one individually.
3. Confess wrong thoughts, words and actions with regard to each son.
4. Ask for forgiveness.
5. Receive forgiveness.
6. Repeat steps 3–5 with God.

1. Talk to Dad about ambivalent feelings for Joseph, resentment of the rest of the family, and personal despair of being recognized for myself.
2. Name and take responsibility for wrong actions, thoughts and words towards Dad.
3. Ask for forgiveness from Dad.
4. Receive forgiveness.
5. Repeat steps 1–4 with other brothers.
6. Repeat steps 1–4 with God.

It makes you gulp a bit to think of doing that kind of thing within your family, doesn't it? It would be extremely demanding and could not be completed in one evening after dinner. It might take weeks (restoring relationships is very hard work), as it could involve much heart-searching. There would probably be failures and a need for further forgiveness and reconciliation; years of lying, hiding and pretending can take months, even years, to recover from. The outcome, however, if a family were to persevere, would be glorious!

The sources of frustration would be removed as each person

- faced up to his responsibility;
- repented; and
- forgave.

As these things happened, the spiritual (and emotional) climate would begin to change; the family would begin to move forward again. The strangleholds of deception and mistrust would be broken. Relationships would begin to function in a healthier way as they were restored and renewed.

The message of hope is twofold: first, that relationships can be transformed by confession and repentance; second, that God has a way of bringing reconciliation to the irreconcilable, even if it takes years to get people's attention.

Reconciliation and the cross

Primarily, a Christian has a responsibility to be obedient to God. This, we have argued, should involve daring prayers of faith. It should also involve following 'leadings from the Lord', 'promptings from the Holy Spirit' or 'hunches' (It depends who you are with, but they all boil down to much the same thing); in other words, responding in faith to guidance. But fundamentally and essentially, obedience means keeping God's law. Nothing else in the life of faith works properly if this simple fact is overlooked.

God's rule about reconciliation, which is at the heart of the gospel, is that we must come in repentance, confessing our sins to him, to receive forgiveness when we have lied, cheated, coveted, or done anything else to breach the 'royal law' as James calls it (James 2:8). Also, Jesus taught us that we have to confess and ask for forgiveness from anyone we have wronged (Matthew 5:23, for example). Merely waiting until the dust has settled and everyone has forgotten about it is not at all the same. Unconfessed sin inevitably brings things to a frustrating standstill in a relationship. But, gloriously, confession and forgiveness bring healing and reconciliation.

Frustration caused by deceit and guilt is ugly, with ugly consequences, but for those who dare to take God's forgiveness and follow his way, that frustration can be replaced by healing and new growth.

Facing responsibility

When it comes to the frustration of relationships that are stagnating because of deceit and guilt, many of us start to develop strong ostrich-like tendencies. We want to avoid conflict and hope the problem will go away. We concentrate on coping with the symptoms rather than curing the disease. We adopt a survival mentality. To change the metaphor, we are content to keep our heads just above the water and never dream that we could ever walk on dry land again. The pagan philosophy of *que será, será*, 'what will be, will be', seems to rule our thinking.

The danger comes when our prayers are completely in the 'coping' mode, as if we have lost our belief in the Lord of heaven and earth 'who is able to do immeasurably more than all we ask or imagine, according to his power that is at work within us' (Ephesians 3:20). We dare not ask or imagine, but we ought to! It is part of our responsibility as followers of Jesus Christ to intercede boldly (like Abraham) for ourselves, other people, and our enemies. It is part of our obedience to him, and expresses our trust in his wisdom and our faith in his power.

So we can pray boldly for circumstances and outcomes to change – for God's Holy Spirit to do the things only he can. We must also put ourselves at his disposal, asking him to show us a way through and a way out. As we do this, we can take up our own responsibility to pray, think through, decide, and act, while still submitting to God's 'Yes', 'No', 'Wait', or whatever else he might say.

It will not have escaped your notice that we believe that personal responsibility, towards God and towards other people, is always an ingredient in times of difficulty, even when a person is thrown into the role of victim. We cannot be held responsible for what other people may say about us or do to us, but we are responsible for what we say or do to them. If we are at fault, we should act.

Here are some statements that may help us break down the frustrating barriers.

'I am sorry that I broke our agreement behind your back by . . .'

'I am sorry that I was unfaithful to you when . . .'

'I am sorry I spent that money without telling you . . .'

'I am sorry that I lied to you about . . .'

'I am sorry that I said . . . about you when you weren't there . . .'

Think seriously about any relationships that may

have reached a frustrating stagnation. Ask God to give you the strength to seek forgiveness and expose any darkness so that the relationship can be healed.

chapter seven

The frustrating years

It may have been the flies that first woke him that morning. Perhaps it was the rats scurrying across the rough blanket at his feet. Whatever it was that roused him, the first thing to strike him was the familiar, pungent smell of urine and faeces. It was this smell that daily shattered any dreams of where he might have been, or of what he might have been doing. It brought him back to reality. He was a prisoner in a rough, eastern gaol, and nobody had told him if he would ever get out. Justice wasn't necessarily a strong point of this country's penal system. Although he was innocent of the crime he had been accused of, he expected to spend a long time in this place, and perhaps, like many others before him, to die here.

And if the smell was the first thing to mock his nose, consciousness soon reminded him of the nagging hunger that had become a constant companion in this awful place. He saw his own body reflected in those other unfortunate 'victims' who either chattered and screamed late into the long nights, or stared blankly through him when he tried to smile. He saw the emaciated skin, the thin limbs, the ribs that could be numbered, the skull beneath the gaunt face, the sore gums, the decaying teeth. There were days when his present position brought him some privileges, but even so, his physical health was deteriorating, and he felt powerless to stop it.

On bad days he grieved about the injustice of it all. It was so unfair. Why should it happen to him? He constantly longed to be free. His dreams were not often dark and bitter. He didn't often want revenge. He just wanted the normal life that everybody else seemed to have. The little things were important as well as the big. He wanted to be able to shop for his own food and choose whom to eat it with. He wanted some control over his own daily existence. And he dared to dream of the big things like a satisfying job, a partner to share his life with as well as his bed, and children to cherish. What was so wrong with that? Was it too much to hope for?

Rejection

For months after his arrival in this place, he had quietly cried himself to sleep. And occasionally, even his sleep seemed tortured. He sometimes woke in a sweat that was more to do with his past than with the humid night air of summer. From deep within him huge sobs surfaced as he tried to obliterate the memory of what his family had done to him. They had certainly contributed to his present mess. Eleven brothers had hated him. God had given him dreams about them, and they didn't like that! Sure, he had been arrogant, and his father weak, but that could never justify what they did to him.

He could still remember the horror of being thrown into the pit, and the smell was worse than prison. He wasn't normally afraid of snakes, but in the pit it was the fear of the unknown. He could remember wondering if he would die from thirst, or from a scorpion sting. The bruises from the slave-traders who pulled him out and silenced his screams remained for days, but the scars from what his family had done wouldn't heal so easily. They were the people who should have protected him, not betrayed him; they should have encouraged and supported him, not abused him. He could remember the years of nastiness and bullying when the playful thump was just too hard, and when things were said or done when his father wasn't around to stop it. His family had excluded him; they wanted him dead. Joseph knew the pain of a rejected child. If only things had been different!

Past mistakes

At times Joseph blamed his family for his pain; at other times he could see his own mistakes and blamed himself. He was frustrated by his own immaturity and mistakes. God was certainly singling him out for something special, but he didn't have to rub it in his brothers' faces. And even though his dad was wrong to favour him so much, he shouldn't have revelled in it when it was obviously causing so much pain in his family. How he had enjoyed it then! If only he hadn't been so naïve and insensitive! He could see that now. The mistakes of his youth had certainly caught up with him. There were times when he longed to be able to change the past, but he knew he couldn't. He could only take responsibility for how he behaved in the present.

Ruined reputation

All that would have been bad enough, but it seemed that whatever he did, he just couldn't win. When he first arrived in Egypt, things could have gone so much worse for him. He could have been dead long ago. But, in a strange way, he could see that God had had his hand on the circumstances, and he had ended up in a very privileged position (as far as slaves go). Potiphar had soon recognized his talent and had trusted him with the running of his household. Through hard work and integrity, he was eventually treated more like a valued servant than a mere slave. He had come to Egypt with nothing, but had gained a reputation. He had come as nobody, and was just beginning to be a somebody, when he again lost everything he had. In honouring God and resisting Potiphar's wife's unsubtle advances, things had got worse. He had been persecuted, for righteousness' sake, and didn't always feel particularly blessed. Why didn't God help him out of his present predicament? He was frustrated by the prison experience that God had allowed.

Being forgotten

And what about his gifts? Why did nobody seem to properly recognize his gifts? His dreams seemed so lucid and the meaning so obvious. Admittedly, he hadn't yet seen some of the earlier interpretations about his family come true, although at the time the interpretation seemed so powerfully clear to him. But the recent ones about the baker and the cupbearer, his prison companions, were accurate. Despite his promises, the cupbearer had forgotten him. And leaving aside the supernatural gifts for a moment, what about his God-given 'natural' abilities? He had the knack of being able to organize things. When he walked into a situation and saw 'what is', he also saw 'what ought to be', and could think of ways for getting from A to B. Potiphar recognized this, and the gaoler gave him opportunity to make things better; but surely God had something more for him than improving the efficiency of an Egyptian gaol? If God hadn't intended him to use his gifts in a more productive way, why had he given him the gifts in the first place? All they were doing were increasing his sense of frustration as he thought about what could have been. He certainly wasn't being used to his full potential in his present situation. And reminding him that Moses would spend forty years in the backside of the desert wasn't any help to him. He couldn't see any way out of his present prison that was restricting him in so many ways. There were too many blocks on what he wanted to do.

And yet . . . and yet there would come a time when he would look at his terrified brothers who feared that he might be about to take his revenge on them, and he would weep for them. Beneath a respectable exterior, this man could have ached with acres of anger; he could have harboured ulcers of unforgiveness; his whole being could have throbbed with boils of bitterness. Instead, he oozes gallons and gallons of grace. He would look them in the eyes and say: 'You intended to harm me, but God intended it for good to accomplish what is now being done, the saving of many lives' (Genesis 50:20). And these are not some trite religious words of a man who doesn't know what he is talking about. They are the words of a man who has been into the darkest tunnel, eventually to see the light at the end of it. He had followed that light and walked into the sunshine. There would come a time when he would recognize that the frustrating years had a purpose.

Out of prison

How did Joseph make that leap from a position of such potential despair to such a bold affirmation of faith? In one sense we shall never know, this side of eternity. We have his words, but we can only guess at his thought processes. We would suggest that in the light of the narrative, most humans would experience something of the range of thoughts and feelings we have described above. But how did he reach his position of peace?

Some may think that it was easy for Joseph because everything worked out for him. He was able to redeem his past mistakes by tremendously significant deeds – 'the saving of many lives'. His physical restrictions were removed. He ended up with a worthwhile job that paid well, a partner, and a family. Some might argue that it is easy to lose your frustrations when you are rich, healthy, loved and important. He reached his peace when his circumstances changed for the better.

It would be foolish to deny that changed circumstances didn't contribute to Joseph's latter peace. But they couldn't have been the sole cause of it, because if they had been, he would still be carrying his frustration and bitterness into his changed environment. He would have achieved much, but would be angry that he hadn't achieved more, and would want revenge for the 'wasted years'. Something happened during his years of imprisonment and slavery that changed his thinking and formed the basis of his ability to turn his back on frustration.

However he experienced it, Joseph must have grown in his understanding of God. Perhaps he had known these things before, but he came to realize them in a new way. They moved from being mere 'precept' to being 'conviction'. And with this conviction in his mind and heart, he was able to rise above the circumstances and ride out the storm as well as the calm.

The sovereign, compassionate, creativity of God

We sometimes linger longer in frustration than we ought to because we lose sight of the creativity of God. We limit God's creative powers to the beginning of time and are blind to what he is always doing.

We have a friend who loves engines. He must have been born in a garage under a bonnet! Whenever our car wouldn't start on a cold winter evening he would come round and fix it. It was so reassuring to stand in the freezing cold in the drive having someone with you who knew what he was doing. God is moved with compassion, and is constantly at our side, even when we do not see it.

Sometimes, even as Christians, we see God as being cold and unfeeling and impotent. 'I mean, it's all right for you, God! It's easy for you to be "Christian". You are the Holy Spirit. You don't have to live down here. You don't have to put up with my family, my loneliness, my job, my unemployment, my children, my childlessness, my physical pain, my emotional hurts.'

We forget that God knows what it is to be born in poverty into a despised and oppressed race. He knows what it is to have the legitimacy of his birth questioned, to have a task so difficult that even his own family and friends thought he was out of his mind, to be betrayed by people he worked with, to face false charges, to be tried by a biased group of people, to be tortured, and to know utter loneliness. When God is with us in our prison, it isn't like having a strange visitor come to see us. He is someone who identifies with our suffering, and wants to help us.

A friend of ours recently wanted to buy his wife a special birthday present, but couldn't think of what to buy. After all, what can you buy a woman who has been twenty-one nineteen times, and who has everything? In the end, he resorted to asking her what she wanted, and to his surprise was told that she wanted a compost bin for the garden. This was duly purchased and installed, and the family now have two rubbish bins in the kitchen: one for rubbish rubbish, and one for compostable rubbish. They now eat the egg and recycle the shell. They creatively use much of what formerly had no value. Each morning our friend lives in terror of being caught by his children accidentally putting the rubbish in the wrong bin!

One of the constant messages of the Bible is that God is so creative, he is able to recycle human rubbish. There is nothing – no person, no set of circumstances, no sin – that he is unable to use creatively to achieve his own purposes. Despite all the evil that his brothers intended for Joseph, despite the failings of Jacob as a father, the failings of Joseph as a family member, the injustice of Potiphar, the lies of his wife, and the neglect of the cupbearer, God was able to use all of that in shaping Joseph and moulding a man whom he would use for his own purposes. Despite all the evil that was thrown at Jesus on the cross, God supremely achieved his own purposes. God doesn't delight in our mistakes, but he isn't phased by them.

If you are anything like us, when the frustrating circumstances pile up, you start to do several things.

- You want God to change the circumstances.
- You may question whether or not you are in the right place, doing the right thing.
- You may wonder whether the difficult circumstances are a satanic attack to discourage you and stop you working for God's kingdom.
- You may wonder if God is punishing you.

The last one is relatively easy to deal with. We know that God isn't punishing us, because he has punished Jesus for our sin and will never punish us. The book of Jonah and the story of the prodigal son are testimonies to the fact that God may sometimes make us face up to the consequences of our actions and may cause our world to fall apart in order to get our attention, but he doesn't punish or destroy. He may chastise us in love (Hebrews 12:4–14), but what else should we expect from a loving Father?

Sometimes we are able to discern why things are happening to us. We feel a strong sense of satanic opposition, or we know that we are being disobedient, and that God is calling us to change. If we know the cause of the frustration, we also know that God is able to stand with us and help us to resist or repent. He is able to creatively use our circumstances to achieve his purposes. But even if we don't know the cause of our present frustrating circumstances, we still know that God is able to stand with us and will work with us to achieve his purposes.

If there is nothing that God cannot use for his glory (and there is *nothing*), we can find peace in frustration. It may be legitimate to look to God to change our circumstances, but if they do not change immediately, or seem as if they are never going to change short of a dramatic miracle, our business is to see how God can creatively use the situation, and us, for his glory.

We may claim to be expert parachutists, but the reality of that claim is tested only when we are thrown from the aeroplane and have to pull the cord and trust the parachute. Our claims to be patient, forgiving, able to cope with conflict, submissive, wise, loving, and able to control our tongues are only really tested in circumstances that are frustrating. It is only in the terror of the free fall that God can teach us about flying.

You may have heard about Joni Eareckson Tada. As a young woman she had a diving accident and became paralysed from the neck down. Her books and films tell of her conversion, her visits to healers, her struggle with frustration, and her acceptance that God was going to use and bless her through her paralysis. Her story isn't glib or trite. We recently saw her at a conference and were aware of how much each day is a still physical struggle for her and her husband. Thousands can testify to being helped by her powerful ministry. And we want to testify how her books have helped us when we have gone through bad times. When it felt as if we were imprisoned with no way out, her message enabled us to focus again on God and gave us hope. Joni's story is powerful and well known, but many other Christians have a similar story.

Sandra was in her late forties. She was a successful business woman with a salary that would have been the envy of many. Four years ago, she woke up one morning with a slight ache in her back. She has never been to work since. She is in constant pain, and cannot sit for long periods or walk reasonable distances. Her condition is deteriorating.

She too has been through the depths of frustration and despair. She worships in a church that teaches that God does heal today (though not on every occasion), and where the church leaders practise what they preach by regularly praying for people to be healed. They have many amazing stories to tell, and they pray regularly for Sandra (with her permission). But, as yet, she has not been healed. Sandra has gone through periods of being angry, bitter, and despondent. Her pain is a constant reminder that she is far from what she would want her physical condition to be. Recently, however, she shared these words:

> I kept asking God why this was happening to me, and I think I know now that he is not going to tell me (in the short term at least). I used to want to be healed and got very bitter when I wasn't. I believe God can heal me. He may do one day. All I can say now is that it isn't important at the moment. I've known God's closeness in this pain in a way which I have never known before. God has forced me to be still, and I've fallen in love with him all over again. I just want to share his grace with others so much. I'm frightened that if I am healed, I might lose this closeness. God really is blessing me so much through this illness.

Sandra isn't a super-spiritual heroine. Those of us who know her admire her down-to-earth view of life. What she can testify to, however, is that there is nothing that God cannot use for his glory. None of us can answer the theological questions surrounding her illness, but on a practical level there are periods when she rises above her frustration by accepting that God is sovereign, that God is compassionate, and that God is so creative, he can use all things for good.

chapter eight

A typical day

A demonstration of power

When Jesus woke up he probably knew that the day had great potential. We know from Mark 7:31 that Jesus had been in the vicinity of Tyre and Sidon and had moved into the region of the Decapolis. He woke this morning in Gentile territory.

For most of his ministry, Jesus had stayed on Jewish soil. He had constantly proclaimed the kingdom of God and done the work of the kingdom. He had healed the sick, raised the dead on occasions, brought good news to the poor, and told people to repent and turn to God. He had forgiven people their sins and proclaimed that religion was not just about ritual, but about relationships with the Father and with each other; it was about changing on the inside as well as on the outside.

Jesus had come to proclaim God's mercy and God's blessing. He was the bread of life, the one person they really needed, regardless of whatever they may have wanted. People who put their trust in him would know a new quality of life now and would live for ever with him. He would sustain them for eternity. It was an exciting time. It was as if God had proclaimed a feast, and had invited everyone to come to the party to feast on him – to know him and to be changed by him.

When, on Jewish soil, Jesus had fed the 5,000 men plus women and children (Mark 6:30–44), he wasn't just feeding hungry people, but was acting out a parable proclaiming God's feast. And with the twelve baskets left over, there was one each for the twelve tribes of Israel.

Now Jesus is on Gentile soil (Mark 8:1–21). He has already revealed the same power. He has driven out a demon and given speech back to a mute. He was greeted with the same kind of amazement that the Jews had shown. And in this region he sets out to teach and heal. He is so amazing and compelling that people stay with him for three days. And this morning when he wakes up he knows there will be another opportunity to act out a parable similar to the one he had enacted on Jewish soil, proclaiming Gods's feast to a Gentile audience. Jesus is the bread of life for both Jew and Gentile.

Jesus teaches the people, he takes the loaves and fishes, he feeds the crowd (about 4,000 men plus women and children), and there are seven baskets left over. (There were seventy Gentile nations, so this may be a symbolic basket for every ten Gentile nations.) And having performed this miracle and enacted the parable, he moves on.

Signs of rejection

Jesus gets into the boat and moves into the region of Dalmanutha. This mission to Dalmanutha might have been as fruitful as any mission, but it starts to spoil the day for Jesus.

He is met by a group of stubborn, argumentative, and unbelieving Pharisees. They ask him for a sign from heaven. Jesus sighs deeply. They have completely missed the point. Where have they been? They ask for a sign, but what about the healings, the deliverances, the nature miracles, the feeding of 9,000 men plus women and children?

Perhaps they are arguing a technical point. Perhaps they will acknowledge that Jesus had given signs on the earth, but want a sign from the heavens. Jesus refuses to pander to their whims. They wouldn't believe a sign from heaven because they hadn't believed the many signs from heaven on earth that had already been given. Indeed, if someone were to rise from the dead, they would not believe. They are far more anxious to collect proof that he is not the Messiah than to listen to evidence that he is.

When the Pharisees ask for a sign, Jesus groans in his spirit. He is frustrated by their unbelief. It grieves him to face such hardness and indifference.

The frustrating disciples

And then, what started out as a good day, but that dipped when Jesus was frustrated by the unbelief of his enemies, gets worse.

Jesus tells the disciples to watch out for the yeast of the Pharisees and that of Herod. The disciples have forgotten to bring bread, and misunderstand Jesus. They think they are being criticized in some way for not having enough food. They have completely misunderstood what has been going on. Jesus is frustrated at their response.

The Son of God is frustrated by his enemies, and frustrated by his friends. Now, of course, some Christians would have told him that his particular emotional response was inappropriate. He should be able to give thanks in all things. They would have told him that if he had had enough faith, that if he was close enough to God, that he had had enough quiet times, that if he was full of the Spirit, somehow the peace of God would have mysteriously dropped out of the sky and would have anaethsetized his emotions, so that he wouldn't feel this frustration.

Of course, they would have been totally wrong. The sinless Son of God shows us by being frustrated twice in one day that there are occasions when it is perfectly legitimate to feel this inward grief and emotional pain when things aren't going the way we would want.

When they reach the other side of the lake, there is an underlying tension that Jesus is sensitive to. There is insecurity in the presence of someone whom they have seen feed 9,000 families. They focus on this one loaf: would it be enough? And perhaps bitterness and condemnation are rising, and accusations about whose fault it was.

There are two types of bread in this story. Jesus is drawing a contrast between the Bread of Life which has been offered to both Jews and Gentiles, and the yeast of the Pharisees.

Yeast is a biblical symbol of sin. Each Passover the Jews had to remove all yeast from their houses, and yeast was not allowed in the offerings. In this context, yeast is referring to the sinful thinking and behaviour of the Pharisees and Herod. It stands for their selfishness, their pretence at real religion, their concern for popular feeling, their arguments and twisted reasoning, and their hardness of heart in the face of adequate testimony (Herod had had the testimony of John the Baptist.)

There are two types of people in this story: one group who ask for signs and will not believe, and one group who have signs, but will not trust.

On at least two previous occasions, Jesus has demonstrated that the disciples could trust him to meet their needs, and on at least two occasions he has demonstrated that they can trust him with their life (Mark 4:35–42; 6:45–52). At the point when they should be encouraged by what God has done, they are brought down to frustration and worry. They can't believe that God will provide. These, who have ministered to others, and who have distributed the miraculous food, are slow to trust that God will provide for themselves.

Jesus gradually leads them from the content of their conversation to their spiritual condition – their spiritual blindness and hardness of heart. He brings to the front of their minds what he had done in the feeding miracles. How can they be anxious about having only one loaf, when with them was the one who had fed 9,000 families with only twelve loaves, leaving nineteen basketfuls over? They have seen his compassion for those in need. Can't they trust him to care for them too?

There is no major catastrophe here, but a conversation about a loaf of bread has shown just how hard their hearts can be, and how blind in their spiritual understanding they are. Unbelief is small, but influential. Jesus is frustrated, not because someone threatens him and makes him feel insecure, and not because someone is disrupting his timetable or making life difficult for him, but because the kingdom of God is being hindered by a lack of faith in those who should know better.

Be encouraged

We've said before that not all frustration is sinful. It's OK to be frustrated for the kingdom of God.

The test of an emotion is not whether it feels

unpleasant or not, but whether it draws us closer to God and his people or away from them. When we are frustrated because God's kingdom is facing resistance, that frustration can cause us to become more dependent on him, and more compassionate towards others.

A degree of frustration in our Christian experience is normal, and a healthy sign of growth. There's no pain in a graveyard, but there is pain in an Olympic stadium as athletes reach for perfection. If you are frustrated because you want to see the kingdom of God growing, be encouraged.

Be encouraged when you are frustrated by the lack of progress you are making in your Christian life. It would be awful if you were complacent about your lack of development. You find yourself longing to know more of what God's Word means. You find yourself discontented with a prayer life that seems so distant and self-centred. You want to be more holy and effective. You find yourself daring to pray: 'Lord, extend the depth and breadth of the ministry you've given me, as you see fit.' Praise God for what his Spirit is doing in your heart, making you frustrated with the *status quo* and moving you to seek something deeper.

Be encouraged too when you feel frustrated by your church. You want something better. If you didn't, there would be something wrong with you. You want to honour God by going for the very best, not just the traditional, the mediocre, or even the good. You look at standards of administration in other institutions and ask 'Why can't we have that in our church?' You look at the best examples of visionary leadership, of human resource management, of financial management, of counselling, of social concern, and of teaching, and you want them for your church. You look at some of the problems and some of the people, and you long for them to change. Just as Paul grieved over Corinth, you may be grieving over your church. But be encouraged. Prophets are rarely happy people. God has moved in your spirit to extend his kingdom. You want to work with him to achieve his purposes. Like you, he wants to establish the best, and root out the worst.

When we look at ourselves and our churches and feel a degree of frustration, we cry out: 'Your kingdom come; your will be done on earth as it is in heaven!' Jesus said we are blessed when we mourn over spiritual failure.

Not only can we be encouraged by the frustration we feel when working for the kingdom, but we should recognize that a degree of it is inevitable.

Christian workers sometimes torture themselves with what they haven't achieved or done for the kingdom. 'If only I was more gifted, more people would have responded . . . if only . . . more would have . . . ' But, look at Jesus. His gifts were perfect, but he was still frustrated by a lack of appropriate response.

In the opening verses of Mark 6, Jesus visits Nazareth, his home territory. This shouldn't be confused with the visit that he had made a year earlier at the very beginning of his ministry, described in Luke 4. At the height of his fame he comes back a second time to give his own people a second chance. But despite this second chance, he is faced with a massive wall of unbelief which has been built up out of jealousy and scepticism. They knew him as an ordinary youngster, and cannot come to terms with the fact that he has outstripped them and that one of their own has an extraordinary and supernatural ministry. John was later to sum it all up by writing: 'He came to his own home, and his own people received him not' (John 1:11, Revised Standard Version). He presents them with truth and expects a positive response, but finds none.

John the Baptist, Jesus's cousin, is beheaded by a fickle ruler. Then Jesus faces the legal trickery of the Pharisees, who try to trap him on questions of cleanness and of honouring parents. They reveal the unbelief behind their demand for a sign. His enemies do not respond positively to his teaching.

Later on that day, Jesus is alone with his disciples and says to them: 'Are you so dull?' They don't respond to him with faith and understanding. At another time, when he tries to tell them some of the most important truths about his forthcoming death, they refuse to believe it, and Peter has to be strongly rebuked (Mark 8:33). In Jesus' parable about the vineyard tenants (Mark 12:1–12), the owner of the vineyard, having seen his servants shamefully treated and killed, contemplates sending the son he loves, and says: 'They will respect my son' (Mark 12:6). But in the short term, it is frustratingly difficult for his son to get a wide hearing. It is no wonder that the verse which is central to the structure of Mark's gospel (and therefore arguably the key verse for the gospel) is Mark 9:7, where God the Father speaks from heaven to a group of disciples around a transfigured Jesus and says: 'This is my Son, whom I love. Listen to him!'

In a sinful world of imperfect understanding and unbelief, a degree of frustration is inevitable for anyone who is serious about building the kingdom.

But frustration should not be an excuse to stop building!

The Bumps Are What You Climb On

Encouragement for difficult days

WARREN W. WIERSBE

'This isn't a path at all,' complains the little girl on the mountain track. 'It's all rocky and bumpy.' Her brother replies, 'Sure, the bumps are what you climb on.'

Christians do not always see the path which God has cleared for us. We face depression, doubt, pain, loneliness and disappointment. We cannot prevent crises from happening but we can use them as stepping-stones to growth.

This is a book of God-given optimism, of new hope for the discouraged.

Inter-Varsity Press

God Isn't in a Hurry

WARREN WIERSBE

'Can't stop', 'In haste', 'Sorry, I've no time . . .'
These all-too-familiar comments pepper our
breathless existence. If we have no time for other
people, do we have time for God, time to grow
spiritually?

In this book Warren Wiersbe, in his usual witty
and pertinent style, leads us gently but firmly
through problems which perplex us all: how to
slow down, suffering, secular fashions, guidance,
the 'me generation', bitterness . . .

Biblical wisdom pervades every page. Take time
to read this book. God will wait for you; he is not
in a hurry.

Warren Wiersbe is a well-known broadcaster in
the USA and a prolific author. He writes from a
warm pastoral heart and a wide knowledge of
Scripture.

Crossway Books

How to Trust God

GARY R MAYES

The hardest thing to do, when confronted with problems, confusion and chaos is – nothing.

Yet Abraham, David, Paul and many other experts in the art of living had to learn to do just that – to wait for God to act, to rest in the hope of his perfect timing, even when time had run out and God's intervention seemed impossible.

This book will help you to trust God, to wait for him and to commit your problems to him, especially when trusting, waiting and committing are the hardest things to do.

Gary R. Mayes is a graduate of Trinity Evangelical Divinity School, Deerfield, Illinois, and pastor of Faith Community Church in Santa Ana, California.

Crossway Books

Secrets of Spiritual Stamina
Work-outs from Colossians
STUART BRISCOE

Do you long for a daily, meaningful relationship with God? One that will sustain you through the good times and the difficult times, and produce an ever-growing faith?

Secrets of Spiritual Stamina provides training for your Christian life, including seventy-two thought-provoking readings on such themes as: Who is Jesus? What is a Christian? Who can I count on? How does my family fit in? What about work? How can I stay on track?

In this book, Stuart Briscoe draws on material from Paul's letter to the Colossians to give you resources for a lifelong, healthy faith.

Stuart Briscoe has worked for thirty-five years with young people, pastors, missionaries and lay leaders in more than 100 countries. He has written many books and, since 1970, has been pastor of Elmbrook Church, Waukesha, Wisconsin.

Crossway Books